Ken Blanchard sai
breakfast of cham
that this is true an
In a world which i
honest and constructive feedback is paramount
to be able to adapt and stay relevant. At Amadeus we have been working with the CALM and CLEAR model as it sets the foundation for an agile and transparent culture.

Sabine Hansen Peck,
Senior Vice President, Human Resources,
Communications & Branding
Amadeus IT Group

In today's world, employee engagement is more important than ever, whether you've been managing virtual, cross-cultural teams around the world or whether you've embarked on your first leadership role. With Feedback First, you gain actionable insights through relevant tips and tools that will help you get results.

Daniel Del Olmo,
President, DineEquity International

FEEDBACK FIRST

Boosting Organisational Performance through CLEAR+CALM Communication

Huibert Evekink with Steven Becker

First Printing, 2016

ISBN: 978-84-617-4618-7

Cover design by Hayder Al-Deen

Illustrations by Huibert Evekink

Formatting by www.indiepublishinggroup.com

For more information, please visit us at www.clearpluscalm.com, or email clearpluscalm@futureteaming.com

To Isabel, Shireen, Diederik, Victoria, Joris, Thomas and Sara

Silence in today's world is deadly. Silence means that good ideas and possibilities do not get addressed.

Prof A.C. Edmondson

ABOUT THE AUTHORS

Huibert Evekink

After growing up in Norway, The Netherlands and Singapore, Huibert studied Business Law and History at Leiden University, in the Netherlands. For 20 years he managed various Sales, Marketing and Human Resource teams for global companies, including Philips, Amadeus and Wyndham Worldwide. Today he is CEO of Futureteaming, a start-up focused on improving performance in teams.

As a follower and a leader he has seen fear stop colleagues from challenging each other. He has also experienced an air of superiority stop managers from listening. The short-term effect of these behaviours is not as deadly as in aviation or healthcare, but in the long run it will bring down any organisation. Therefore, as head of culture and engagement for a global IT company, he developed a unique feedback programme to train team members and their leaders to give and receive feedback effectively. It took time and dedication, but engagement and performance improved dramatically.

The INSEAD Business School in France gave him an opportunity to combine practical experience with the theory of human behaviour and the—often hidden—dynamics of organisations. The Consulting and Coaching for Change Masters programme (CCC) integrates business education with a range of psychological disciplines. His thesis research on battling isolation in virtual teams concluded that regular feedback—preferably face to face—is key to personal wellbeing and high performance.

During his work as a ski guide/mountaineer he experienced first-hand how good communication can also mean the difference between success and disaster in harsh alpine environments. A good technical instructor will lead the way and hopefully keep you safe. A great guide will do the same AND give you feedback to make you a better skier and mountaineer. Much like his business partner and co-author Steven Becker piloting an aluminium tube at 30,000 feet, the best guides combine technical and non-technical skills to safely manage—and learn from—complex situations.

Steven Becker

Steven has worked as a KLM Royal Dutch Airlines Co-pilot and Captain for the last 23 years. He also became an instructor and examiner early on, which resulted in a situation unique in the Aviation Industry: First Officers examining Captains during Proficiency Checks.

Today, Steven is Captain on the Airbus A330 and co-founder of Futureteaming, after setting up several companies focused on improving team performance in organisations using his Crew Resource Management (CRM) expertise.

Modern airlines deploy this 'non-technical' programme to train their crews to speak up when a situation arises which threatens safety or efficiency. After the introduction of the jet engine, about 60% to 80% of incidents and accidents in civil aviation are now caused by human error: ineffective communication, poor decision-making and ineffective leadership. CRM helps crew members challenge authority and push for solutions they feel are best, even when it involves disagreement. Failing to speak up can have serious career consequences in aviation, regardless of rank, age, gender and seniority. Research shows that pilots have about half as much conflict as people in other organisations because they train in feedback techniques that keep arguments factual, respectful and focused on learning.[1]

Not surprisingly, Crew Resource Management has also reached beyond the cockpit into improving teamwork and leadership in other industries. The pressure to operate safely and economically in an extreme environment has produced expertise that other teams can use to manage stress and complexity.

Steven and his colleagues around the world have learned, often the hard way, that soft skills are just as important as technical skills.

TABLE OF CONTENTS

INTRODUCTION

If we want things to stay as they are, everything will have to change.

Tomasi di Lampedusa

THE OLD MILITARY acronym VUCA has become a trendy management term to describe the volatile, uncertain, complex and ambiguous future that organisations will have to survive and prosper in. Change itself is nothing new, but the relentless speed of innovation and the number of global trends playing a role have dramatically increased. Long-term term planning is being replaced by real-time learning and adaptation. Tomorrow's organisations—and the people in them—will have to be more flexible and agile than ever before.

We believe continuous feedback is the starting point for performance in a dynamic world. It connects minds so they can learn and collaborate. It shapes behaviour and opens the door to better things. If we cannot question each other's mistakes in a factual and respectful manner, most change initiatives are doomed from the start: we continue to make the same errors over and over again.

The youngest and already the biggest, generation in the workplace, the Millennials or Generation Y, sees instant feedback—giving and receiving—as the only way to advance. Less intimidated by status and raised on social media, they crave comments and 'likes', processing information much faster than older generations. In the absence of regular progress updates, younger team members rapidly lose their motivation as they realise they have no idea what to start, continue or stop doing. Older generations often complain about this 'impatience', but we had better find a way to deal with it if we want top talent to stick around.

Sounds sensible, but what do we mean by feedback?

> Feedback is information we give and receive about actual and ideal behaviour, with the intention of improving it.

This focus on positive growth makes feedback one of the most important—and difficult—forms of communication. It is not only sharing information or proving a point. It is not just telling people what to do. It is not only demonstrating a potential opportunity or problem. The final goal of feedback is to improve performance; without this developmental step, we are simply talking about criticism, blaming or punishing.

So, if feedback is the breakfast of champions, then how come we have all been faced with silence or upsetting feedback—sometimes to the point of being counterproductive? The answer is simple: giving feedback can be a risky business; it can trigger conflict and it might even get you fired. To avoid problems, we tell white lies or say nothing, seeking safety in silence.

If we do speak up, feedback is rarely received with open arms. Without the capacity to listen and reflect on feedback, nothing changes for the better.

The Dramatic Consequences of Poor Feedback

The Gallup engagement survey asks employees twelve simple questions—the Q12—of which nine are directly or indirectly related to feedback, covering topics like recognition, regular progress updates, sharing and evaluating opinions, trusting relationships, etc. In their 2016 Meta-analysis[2] of the relationship between engagement and business performance, Gallup reviewed 339 studies across 230 organisations in 49 industries, with 1,882,131 employees in 73 countries. This research clearly showed that teams with low engagement—and therefore little to no effective feedback—also scored low on the following business metrics:

- Lower customer loyalty.
- Lower profitability.
- Lower productivity.
- Higher turnover.
- Poor ethical standards and behaviour.
- Higher quality defects.
- Poor safety practices and records.

The really shocking fact is that only 13 % of employees worldwide are engaged in their jobs, according to the Gallup Report on the State of the Global Workplace[3]. Gallup calculates that the 'disengagement cost' to the US alone amounts to between $450 billion to $550 billion per year.[4] US Millennials are the least engaged generation and only 19% say they receive feedback on a regular basis.[5]

Unsurprisingly, years of research across the globe clearly shows that innovation and learning in organisations depend on the ability to give AND receive quality feedback.[6]

Despite the mounting evidence that skilled feedback produces high performance—and silence results in underperforming workplaces with unhappy customers—few organisations target feedback as a development area. Closing the feedback loop is what inspired us to write *Feedback First.*

The Winning Formula: CLEAR+CALM

In our work with clients we always start with feedback as the basis for change; it is the glue that holds everything together. Working on any improvement without the ability to talk is a waste of time.

Therefore, we developed a unique framework for giving and receiving feedback: the CLEAR+CALM model.

We will discuss these acronyms in detail, but in short:

- CLEAR: Be factual and focused on improvement when giving feedback.
- CALM: Stay cool to listen, question and improve.

CLEAR+CALM = FEEDBACK THAT WORKS

Cross Industry Innovation: Learning from Each Other

By combining our experience in aviation and multinational organisations with specific feedback research, we developed guidelines for behaviour that work: the dos and don'ts of feedback.

The model covers five steps for giving and four for receiving, feedback effectively and respectfully—up, down and peer-to-peer. The behaviour in the CLEAR+CALM model is evidence-based, observable, measurable and trainable.

Who Should Read *Feedback First*? Everybody!

- Leaders who want to create a feedback culture in their organisations—small, big, locally or globally.
- Teams who want to improve performance by building feedback into their daily work practices: from high-risk teams to high-tech teams.
- Anyone who wants to become a more assertive and effective communicator and listener, regardless of rank or position.
- Academics who are studying the subject.
- Consultants who help companies and teams to change and perform better.

Conclusion: The Future Starts with Feedback

FEEDBACK FIRST: Boosting Organisational Performance through CLEAR+CALM Communication is the ultimate guide to improving performance through effective feedback. It gives everybody in the organisation a voice, as well as the skills and confidence to speak up. On the receiving end, this book helps team members find the courage to listen and improve, regardless of rank, culture, gender or age. In short, *FEEDBACK FIRST* provides the feedback infrastructure needed for any type of change. No feedback, no learning, no improvement, no future—it's that simple.

The CLEAR+CALM model will show you how to:

- Understand the dynamics of feedback across hierarchies and cultures.
- Create a safe environment for speaking up and listening.
- Be factual when giving feedback.
- Stay calm in order to listen, question and improve.
- Agree and follow up on actions.

Good luck!

Throughout this Book, We Will Use the Following Feedback Terms:

- Feedback can be given or received. Consequently, we will use the terms 'giver' and 'receiver' to refer to each party and alternate the use of the pronouns 'he' or 'she'.

- Feedback can be positive—to recognise and reinforce good behaviour, or it can be more critical or developmental in nature—to improve behaviour. The latter is by far the most complex and therefore covers the main part of the book. We will use 'feedback' and 'positive feedback' to distinguish between the two.

- Feedback can be divided into informal, regular feedback and more formal types of feedback that are typically shared during performance reviews.

- Feedback can be unsolicited or specifically asked for.

PART I: THE THEORY OF FEEDBACK

1

THE DYNAMICS OF FEEDBACK

Understanding evolves through three phases: simplistic, complex and profoundly simple.

William Schultz

'SO, WHEN YOU compliment Saanvi for organising a great event, she gets a little shot of a brain chemical called dopamine. This dopamine produces a feeling of joy and motivates her to keep doing a great job. You see, it makes perfect business sense to recognise our team members!' My class of Asian managers nodded and made some notes.

Five years ago I developed a 'people skills' course to help leaders run their teams more effectively. We invited managers from all functions, regions and levels, with many of them coming from an engineering background, where emotional intelligence was not part of the menu.

During the first sessions the participants remained silent and visibly bored. In the course feedback—unsurprisingly—I got low marks as the leaders rated the experience as a waste of valuable time: too soft, too vague, too wishy-washy. So I decided to make the 'soft' into 'hard' by going back to the basics: what drives behaviour? If I could prove that there is science behind the way humans think, feel and act maybe my logically-minded colleagues would enjoy the course more. The next session I started out talking about evolution, fight or flight, human biases, universal drives, cultural norms, neuroscience and much, much more. It worked! Spontaneous discussions erupted, as people started making the links with their daily work and even their private lives. Human behaviour suddenly became understandable and interesting. Some participants even started reflecting on their own attitude.

Once we reached a good level of theoretical understanding, I finished with steps, tips and tricks, which now made more sense. People could easily remember them and—more importantly—use them in a flexible way to improve team engagement and performance.

My takeaways from five years from giving courses to hundreds of managers around the world:

1. Most of us have a rather simplistic and judgemental view of other people. He is bad, she is smart, they are lazy, the Dutch are cheap, women are emotional, men cannot multi-task, marketers are liars and software developers are nerds.

Ignorance is bliss because it allows us to quickly make sense of the world, without having to worry about inconvenient facts.

2. To understand and manage human behaviour you need to question your assumptions, starting with the word 'why'. Once you have a solid understanding of human behaviour, then steps, hacks and checklists can help you to remember and apply deeper knowledge: tips make life a bit simpler.

3. Tips without deeper understanding are too simplistic to be useful. Based on the number of 'life hacks' we consume on a daily basis, you would expect us all to be much better leaders, parents, partners and professionals; however, such shortcuts don't work.

   A pilot can teach you how to fly using a simulator in a couple of hours; trust me, I managed to take-off, cruise and land in stable conditions. Then my instructor simulated an engine fire and I was immediately in trouble because I did not have the knowledge, training or experience to adapt to the emergency situation. Managing yourself and other people's behaviour is a bit like flying and—unfortunately—many of us struggle to keep the plane in the air.

We, the authors, believe that every part of our character, background, social context and traditions has a crucial impact on how we give and receive feedback. So before we introduce our CLEAR+CALM method, this chapter will give you the necessary insights to understand and manage the dynamics of feedback.

It's All About Behaviour

In his book *Cultures and Organizations,* Geert Hofstede, the 'godfather' of cultural studies, describes three different 'software programs' that drive human thinking and behaviour: personality, culture and human nature.[7] The problem with some of this mental software is that it may have worked well in the past but it has never been updated to deal with the present or future.

- **Human nature** is what all of us have in common, from Iceland to Bora Bora. It's hardwired into our brains, forming a universal 'operating system'. We all feel fear, shame, anger, joy and sadness. We are all attracted and submissive to power. We all want to belong to a tribe. We are all highly sensitive to fairness: 'I'll scratch your back if your scratch mine'. We all want to be loved and our sense of empathy drives us to care about the people around us. However, what we do with these drives and feelings—how we express emotions like fear, joy and anger—is influenced by culture and personality.
- **Culture** is made up of unwritten laws and values

that we learn in our social environment: 'the way we do things around here'. We tend to judge 'the way they do things around there' by our own cultural norms and usually not for the better. The conflict between groups over religious beliefs, political values and behavioural norms is sadly a part of our daily lives.

- **Personality** is unique to every individual. It is shaped by distinctive character traits that are partly inherited (nature) and partly modified by culture and experience (nurture).

By themselves, human drives, culture and personality are complex topics and often quite difficult to understand. Mix them together and you can end up with a big knot that would take years—if ever—of study and experience to untangle.

However, a basic knowledge of mental software is a good starting point to understanding and managing the dynamics of feedback.

Human Nature and Feedback

Human nature refers to the drives and instincts which we tend to have naturally, independent of our personality and cultural influences. It includes ways of thinking, feeling and acting.

In their books *Driven* and *Driven to Lead*, Harvard Professors Paul Lawrence and Nitin Nohria take years of research from the different social sciences and neuroscience to provide a powerful explanation for the origins of human behaviour.[8] They propose four innate, independent human drives that shape our social behaviour and the choices we make:

1. A drive to acquire and control goods and experiences that improve our status in relation to others.
2. A drive to bond with others in caring relationships.
3. A drive to learn and make sense of the world.

4. A drive to defend ourselves, our loved ones, beliefs and material possessions.

The underlying logic is that all four drives improve our odds of passing our genes on to the next generation.

Now let's apply these drives to feedback in an organisational setting:

Drive 1. A Drive to Acquire and Control: Keeping the Boss Happy

Organisations offer the perfect environment for this drive to flourish as we compete and compare for resources—money—and status. It's in our genes to fight for power and to submit to authority, starting with the respect we (must) show for our parents. Lack of power generates fear of losing one's job, of not getting that promotion, of humiliation and this angst is often used to reinforce systems of hierarchy.

On the other hand, having the power can lead you to

overestimate your impact and superiority. Leaders, as they gain power, often feel an increasing distance and difference between themselves and their followers. This process of 'dehumanization' deprives followers of human qualities and reduces both the ability to empathise and the willingness to tune into the opinion of colleagues lower in rank. Leaders can become cruel, corrupt and detached from reality. Open any history book and you see this same story unfolding time and time again. Distance in combination with authority can lead to disaster: dictatorial leadership with brutal oppression.

Power Tends to Corrupt

In a fascinating experiment, the HEC business school of Lausanne set up lab experiments where participants played a dictator game. Leaders had to decide how to divide the money between themselves and their teams.

Results showed that leaders with more followers, or higher power leaders, took more of the money, and high levels of testosterone made the corruption worse.[9] Testosterone, a hormone found in men and women, prepares us for danger and competition, increasing fearlessness and risk taking, while lowering empathy and social behaviour. Men produce ten to twenty times as much of it as women. Not surprisingly, a study by the World Bank concludes that a higher rate of female participation in government is associated with lower levels of corruption.[10] We can safely assume the same for companies and other organisations.

By its very nature, hierarchy dramatically reduces the desire of those lower down to speak up and those higher up to listen. In many organisations, it is a basic survival strategy to inflate the degree to which you agree with your superiors. Managers reinforce this behaviour by, unconsciously, looking for an endorsement of their views, rather than honest questioning or critical feedback. The danger with flattery is that it cuts them off from the facts.

Under these circumstances, it is not hard to understand that feedback can become a risky business. Despite the proven benefits of speaking up, employees often remain silent out of a combination of fear, respect and even childlike admiration for the person in power. The world of work is littered with organisations—NASA's Discovery Space Shuttle explosion, South Yorkshire Police's Hillsborough football disaster, Enron's accounting scandals, Lehman Brothers' investment strategy, the BP oil spill and Volkswagen TDI—that drove themselves and their surroundings, into the ground, because team members and peers did not feel safe to challenge their misguided or corrupt leaders.

While there has been a growing trend toward more participative work relationships and practices, feedback is still something that usually happens from the top down: from the powerful to the powerless.

Power Play at The Royal Bank of Scotland

It was the biggest financial time bomb in history, and it took £45 billion of taxpayer's money to bail out the Royal Bank of Scotland.

The incredible growth of RBS took place over a 10-year period and was led by CEO Fred, 'the Shred', Goodwin and his Board. As the credit crunch was tightening its grip on the financial markets in 2007, Goodwin led a $100 billion takeover of Dutch rival ABN Amro, stretching RBS's capital reserves to the limit and ultimately bringing RBS down.

In his Financial Times article 'A Culture Ratio is More Important than a Capital Ratio' Simon Samuels compares how three pairs of Banks, similar in capital strengths, survived the financial crisis: Citigroup and JPMorgan Chase; RBS and Barclays: Fortis and BNP Paribas.[11] Citi, RBS and Fortis needed the taxpayers to step in; the others did not. Samuels concludes that the determining factor was not the capital levels, but the feedback culture. In RBS the directors of the board were experienced and qualified bankers, but they did they not stand up to authority. Apparently, the culture was not one that encouraged challenge and feedback. The board felt intimidated by Goodwin and did not challenge him or each other.

The UK's 2009 Walker Report on Corporate Governance explicitly recommends that directors should be ready, able and encouraged to challenge and test proposals on strategy put forward by the CEO. They should satisfy themselves that board discussion and decision-making on risk matters is based on accurate and appropriately comprehensive information and draws on external analysis and input.[12] On 21 July 2016, 13 of America's heavyweight CEOs (e.g. GM, GE, JPMorgan, Berkshire Hathaway), worried about big business popularity being at an all-time low, released a report called Commonsense Corporate Governance Principles, containing 77 suggestions for how big companies should be led, how they should communicate with their shareholders, and how large investment firms should fulfil their own responsibilities.[13] Several recommendations mention feedback:

'Directors should be strong and steadfast, independent of mind and willing to challenge constructively but not be divisive or self-serving. Collaboration and collegiality also are critical for a healthly, functioning board'.[14]

Drive 2. A Drive to Bond: Nurturing Relationships

The drive to bond is the reason we build and nurture strong relationships with individuals and groups around us. If the first drive is all about 'me', the second drive promotes the 'we'. Our drive to build and maintain caring relationships with others may stop us from asking for feedback or giving advice. Since we don't want to be perceived as ignorant, cruel or superior we withhold—or water down—our feedback.

For the receiver, threatening feedback can provoke deep feelings of fear, rejection and ridicule: our status in the group is under attack. We may look for feedback to learn, but often interpret the response as evidence that we are unloved or disrespected. From an evolutionary standpoint, being an outcast is fatal. To protect ourselves from this feedback-related anxiety, we have a tendency to absorb feedback that makes us feel good and filter out what we don't like. We are often not aware of this selection process.

In close-knit teams, we may feel additional pressure to avoid raising ‘controversial’ issues or alternative solutions to maintain harmony. This psychological phenomenon is called group-think and it produces an increased certainty that the right decision has been made, without considering new facts or alternative solutions.

Drive 3. A Drive to Learn: Convincing Ourselves that We Are Always Right

The drive to explore and find meaning should naturally promote feedback, but more often it produces defensive reactions—that is if new information clashes with what we already think or believe about others, the world and ourselves. Here, we enter into the field of universal biases and stereotypes—predetermined mental notions and beliefs—that lead us to follow a quasi-logical route to form opinions about others, usually not for the better.

A bias is a term used to describe a preference towards a particular perspective, ideology or result, especially when prejudice makes it hard to be impartial or objective.

A **stereotype** is a preconceived idea that attributes certain characteristics to all the members of a group. The term often has a negative meaning when referring to an oversimplified, exaggerated, or demeaning assumption.

If you think that all Asians are smart, or white men can't dance, that is a stereotype. But if you hired a man for a job when you interviewed an equally qualified woman because you think women are not as decisive as men, you are biased.

Most biases (of which there are plenty) can be traced back to the confirmation bias or the tendency to seek and find confirmatory evidence to 'prove' pre-existing beliefs and to ignore or rationalise away disconfirming evidence. I can think of several colleagues who, once they make up their mind about someone, will always find evidence to support their—first—impression, no matter what happens. With them you are forever blessed or doomed. We fail to see that the truth is just one version of reality: our story, featuring ourselves in a heroic role. We find it hard—or even impossible—to understand and accept that others are living their own adventure.

Let's have a look at some of the most important biases:

'You Are the Problem' Bias **(aka Fundamental Attribution Bias)**

We typically attribute others' problematic behaviour to their poor attitude or personality, rather than look at their circumstances. As such, it is not entirely strange that feedback can come across as a personal attack or character assassination. We do exactly the opposite when we blame our own failures on the circumstances of the situation.

'My Universal Truth Bias' **(aka Naive Realism Bias)**

We tend to see our world as the only objective truth. This reality is so 'naturally obvious' that we cannot imagine any other points of view, unless we are dealing with irrational people. When we give feedback, therefore, we often fail to explain our arguments with clear examples.

Paranoia Bias (aka Negativity Bias)

Research shows that we pay more attention to negative feedback than we do to positive feedback.[15] We remember negative comments more than praise and we can dwell compulsively on critical remarks even if they're buried beneath heaps of compliments.

'I Am Above Average' Bias (aka Self-Serving Biases)

Self-serving biases lead us to be over-optimistic about our own behaviour and achievements. In other words, we see ourselves through rose-coloured glasses. These positive self-perceptions keep us motivated and productive, but they also prevent us from recognizing that we are sometimes wrong. Therefore, it is no wonder that so many people brush others' critical feedback off as inaccurate and only look for evidence to confirm their desired state. Lying to yourself destroys the possibility of learning.

We are good at spotting these self-serving biases in others, but it is hard to accept that we have them too: 'Other people might be biased, but I am obviously above average!'

By understanding some of these universal bias dynamics, both the receiver and the giver can take a more informed and constructive approach to feedback.

'Don't confuse me with the facts'

In their book *Partisan Hearts and Minds,* political scientists Donald Green, Bradly Palmquist, and Eric Schickler demonstrated that most people do not vote for a political party for its position on specific political issues—like healthcare or climate change. Instead, we support a political ideology, usually inherited from our parents or friends during our upbringing. Once we identify with the left, the right—or anything in between—the confirmation bias helps us find evidence to confirm our deeper political beliefs and—unconsciously—rationalise away claims that may clash. Politicians know how to sell big ideas and get votes, regardless of the facts. The claims that helped the United Kingdom to Brexit were either wrong or impossible to predict. Spend some time on www.fact-check.org, a website that aims to reduce the level of deception in U.S. politics, and you will see that what politicians say and claim is increasingly 'factless'.

Another example of hanging on to deep beliefs is the right to bear firearms as protected in the Second Amendment to the United State Constitution of 1789. Mass shootings are used by the anti-gun supporters as an argument for restricting the sales of firearms, while the pro-gun lobby reframes the same sad events in order to push gun ownership for self-defence. Sure enough, their strategy seems to work: gun purchases and gun stock prices go up after mass shootings.

Drive 4. A Drive to Defend: Fight or Flight

As human beings, we have an innate drive to defend our valued achievements, belongings, status, relationships and beliefs. Remember that the words used in feedback can feel just as threatening as physical danger: mental pain hurts too. Threat triggers defensiveness and as a result, we either attack or retreat. As we can see around us every day, much of human activity is provoked by this drive.

In his book *The Chimp Paradox,* Dr Steve Peters gives an easy way to understand how the mind works.[18] His 'Chimp Management' model is made up of the Chimp (frontal brain), The Human (limbic brain) and the Computer (parietal brain) to form the psychological mind. These brains are supposed to work together but often fight for control, especially in times of perceived danger and stress.

Apply this model to receiving negative feedback and

most of us have experienced the 'inner discussions' of the human and the chimp.

The Human

When we have time and feel relaxed we explore for facts. We look for evidence to support our arguments and offer fair feedback. Like scientists, we investigate the context of the situation and the people involved.

Human Thinking

- Realising that opinions are not facts: we can truly only see our own reality.
- Building arguments using evidence.
- Avoiding rationalising away uncomfortable facts and events to protect our image and self-esteem.

- Showing empathy for people around us.
- Focusing on compromise and mutually beneficial solutions to problems.
- Understanding that humans make mistakes and nobody is perfect.

The Monkey

The monkey symbolises our emotional machine. In milliseconds the brain can process thoughts and feelings that are triggered by danger or opportunity. Some emotions are automatic and unconscious, like fear of snakes; some translate into conscious feelings—anger, shame, love and happiness. Emotions keep us safe and give our lives meaning and value.

Monkey Thinking

- Jumping to conclusions.
- Acting impulsively before thinking things through.

- Being paranoid and suspicious of others ('They are out to get me', 'Trust nobody').
- Focusing excessively on negative feedback and ignoring the positive ('Better safe than sorry').
- Having catastrophic thoughts ('It will all go wrong').
- Black-and-white thinking ('He is evil' or 'You are for or against me').

This 'shoot-first-ask-questions-later' attitude keeps us safe in dangerous situations, but it is often inappropriate in normal organisational life.

Monkey Attack

My friend Anna uses the monkey to describe how she sometimes feels after receiving critical feedback: 'My monkey was jumping all over the place after David told me the numbers in the budget were wrong' or 'I was dealing with a paranoid monkey when Marit didn't reply to my mail'. Anna cleverly uses the mental picture of a monkey to name the emotion (anger, fear, jealousy) to control her reactions. She also knows that the thoughts and reactions of the monkey do not define her as a person, but that she is responsible for calmly dealing with her impulses before they deal with her.

Fight or Flight

If your monkey feels your sense of safety or status is under massive attack, it will become angry and fearful, making you aggressive or submissive to the dominant person. Once your 'fight or flight' instincts have hijacked your brain, it is difficult to think straight and learn.

In response to milder threats, we use coping mechanisms that help us deal with unpleasant—and often conflicting—thoughts, feelings and behaviours.[19] In psychology, this type of mental stress is called 'cognitive dissonance'. If I see myself as a highly distinguished expert, a mistake can me feel incompetent and foolish. To reduce the mental stress, the brain will reframe the situation in my favour and rationalise away the inconvenient evidence.

Some of the ways in which we unconsciously defend ourselves against negative feedback are:

1. Refusing to accept reality or facts. We act as if a painful event did not happen or deny that it is actually a failure.

2. Downplaying the importance or impact of the feedback. We can also pretend we simply do not care what others think of us.
3. Coming up with convenient excuses. We blame others to counter critical feedback.
4. Questioning the credibility or intentions of the giver of feedback. From where we're standing, it looks like the giver lacks the skills or the right intentions to comment.

I have always been surprised at how creative people are when it comes to making up excuses for mistakes or poor performance, even if the evidence speaks for itself. After hours of pointless discussions, you could easily come to the conclusion that the receiver of feedback is either delusional or evil.

Today I understand that we are not always aware of

the defences we put up to protect ourselves. Some mistakes are just too painful to accept, so our brains block them out. The longer the discussion drags on, the more we dig in and the harder it becomes to admit we might be wrong. To make matters worse, specialists and leaders—smart, admired and powerful—have the most to lose from mistakes and therefore often filter out failure. Learning is sacrificed for ego, without even realising it.

Making the Same Mistakes...Over and Over Again

Johns Hopkins Hospital patient safety experts have calculated that more than 250,000 patients die every year due to medical error, making it the third biggest killer in the United States—behind heart disease and cancer. Matthew Syed, in his book *Black Box Thinking: The Surprising Truth About Success*, explains that healthcare does not learn from failure. Making mistakes is considered unprofessional and therefore highly threatening to ego and reputation.[20] Mistakes are filtered out, and therefore made over and over again.

In the aviation industry the feedback culture enables crews to learn from errors, rather than being threatened by them. Team members are not intimidated about admitting mistakes because they know errors contain valuable information to improve safety and efficiency.

Many businesses, government organisations, security forces and hospitals, are starting to introduce feedback to learn from mistakes.

Culture and Feedback

Most of us are socialised to view the world from a national perspective. This deep and invisible programming starts early on in the family and continues in the neighbourhood, schools and the workplace. Because culture is so close to us—a part of us, if you will—we're somewhat blind to the effects it has on us. It is like wearing red, white and blue coloured sunglasses and thinking other countries are just better or lesser versions of, in this case, Holland. National culture subconsciously affects the way we think, feel and act at home and in the office.

Despite living most of my life outside the Netherlands, the Netherlands very much lives inside me: I still see the world through filtered glasses, whether I like it or not.

However, after a lot of mistakes, reflection and immersion, I have become more culturally empathic. I can step back and imagine how people from certain other cultures might feel. That does not mean I always agree with local ways of thinking or doing things, but I can at least take them into account before passing judgement or withholding it altogether.

Culture can be a sensitive topic. We are all the same species, but every individual is different. Some people feel that focusing on cultural differences can lead us to stereotype and put individuals in boxes. Another hot topic is what I call, '*Who are you to talk about my mother?*' *syndrome*. I can be critical of the Dutch, but I can easily become defensive if I feel someone from a different culture is judging my country. This syndrome is a normal group phenomenon called the 'intergroup sensitivity effect'.[21]

Cross-cultural Feedback

National cultures deeply impact the way we communicate and therefore, the way we give and receive feedback. Effective feedback in a single culture can often prove quite challenging; feedback across cultures is even more complex. Cross-cultural awareness and experiences can significantly improve our relationships and communication, but it is impossible to master every feedback style. We would need to speak hundreds of languages fluently AND know the cultural context. The cultural immersion required would be interesting, but highly impractical in an organisational setting.

Let's have a look at some of the differences in feedback orientation across cultures, using the Rolls Royce of culture studies: The Global Leadership and Organizational Behaviour Effectiveness (GLOBE) Study.[22] Using the research data from 17,000 middle managers, a team of

170 researchers worked together to study the societal, culture and organisational culture and attributes of effective leadership in 62 countries. Based on the work of Hofstede and others they developed eight more criteria to help profile countries in a consistent manner:

- Performance Orientation.
- Future Orientation.
- Gender Egalitarianism.
- Assertiveness.
- Individualism and Collectivism.
- Power Distance.
- Human Orientation.
- Uncertainty Avoidance.

From this academic study, we have chosen four dimensions that are particularly important when it comes to managing feedback: assertiveness, collectivism, gender egalitarianism and power distance. You can find a complete overview of the scores and tips on how to deal with different feedback styles, on **futureteaming.com/culture-feedback-tool.** This app was built together with our data analytics partner Conento.

Assertiveness

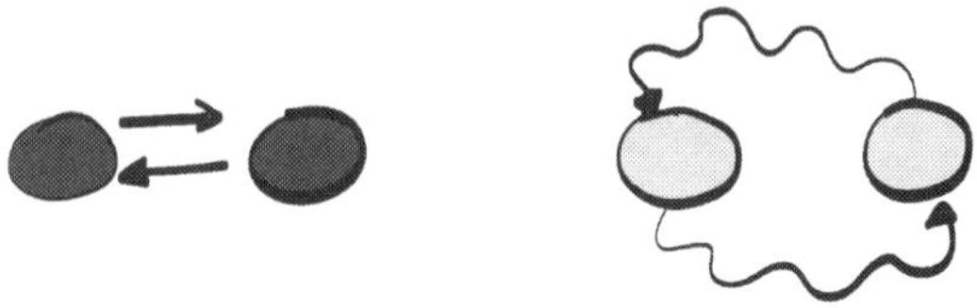

Assertiveness is the degree to which individuals are assertive, confrontational and aggressive in their relationships with others.

- In highly assertive cultures like Germany, the United States and Turkey, social courtesies are rarely required before getting to the point. Summaries and repetition are appreciated in conversation, as they clarify the communication between both parties. Furthermore, negative feedback is to be provided frankly, bluntly and honestly. Negative messages stand alone and do not need to be softened by positive ones. Assertive cultures use absolute descriptors like 'totally unacceptable' or 'completely unprofessional' and criticism may be given in front of a group.
- In unassertive cultures like Sweden, Switzerland and New Zealand, negative feedback is provided softly, subtly and diplomatically. Messages are ambiguous, implied but not plainly expressed. Qualifying descriptors are often used ('a bit', 'slightly', 'somewhat') during criticism. Feedback is almost always a

private affair. Feedback can feel uncomfortable and can easily be seen as judgmental.

I will never forget my first big presentation to a group of German colleagues in Frankfurt. From the start the audience started asking questions in a very negative, confrontational and aggressive way. I managed to get through the ordeal thinking I had deeply disappointed everyone. When my German colleagues came up to greet me later I told them about my experience. They were surprised and explained they were simply testing my thinking. They told me I defended my arguments well and the presentation was credible and appreciated. I have been through the same process in France—unnerving until you understand what is going on.

Collectivism

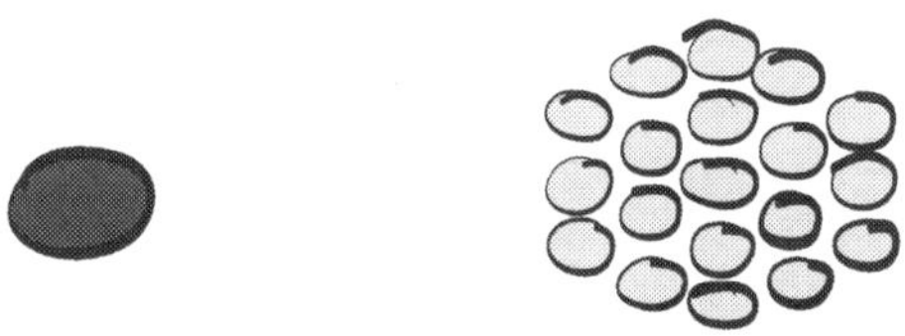

Individual and collective dimensions measure the degree to which people express pride, loyalty and cohesiveness with their organisations or families.

- In individualist cultures like Canada, England and Finland, there is a focus on individuals and personal goals and achievements. Uniqueness and self-determination are valued concepts. A person is admired if they are self-made; if they show initiative and work well independently. Feedback tends to be individualised and direct in the professional relationship.

- In collectivist cultures like India, Iran and Singapore, there is a collective, shared identity and a strong focus on harmony and group achievements. Feedback is more group-focused and less direct. If you fail, you fail the group and losing face in front of the group is to be avoided at all costs.

After presenting in Frankfurt, I jumped on a plane to give the same presentation to my colleagues in Bangkok. Now I went from extreme confrontation to exactly the opposite. Few people in the audience would question what I presented or react to any of my invitations to speak up. However, group exercises were completed and presented with great enthusiasm. After the presentation, everyone smiled, thanked me and walked away, leaving me hungry for more feedback.

Gender Egalitarianism

One of the most fundamental ways societies differ is in the way they view the proper roles for—and relationships between—women and men. Some cultures believe that men and women are equal and suited to the same functions, both at work and at home. Less egalitarian societies believe that women have a different status than men and should take different roles. Societies that score low on gender egalitarianism promote relationships where men control women.

Scholars from various fields agree that the origins of the difference between men's and women's roles can be found in biology: women not only deliver children but also feed and nurture them.[23] So, we have developed a universal view that responsibility for taking care of people generally falls on women and men are in charge of providing—and often competing for—resources.

Stereotypes about what social roles are permitted for males and females influence participation in the labour market and contribution to family life. Gender inequality at home, in the workplace and society reinforce stereotypes, bringing us full circle: what you see is what you get and what you get is what you see.

Gender egalitarianism influences the way women give and receive feedback.

- In societies that score high on gender egalitarianism like Hungary, Denmark and Namibia, women are more likely to give feedback using their local feedback style as they actively participate in the labour force in positions of authority and decision-making. That is not to say woman do not suffer gender discrimination as access to top jobs and equal pay are hot topics in even the most egalitarian societies.

- In societies that score lower on gender egalitarianism, like Kuwait or South Korea, fewer women work. The ones that do work have less authority and status than men and tend to cluster in jobs deemed suitable for women, also known as 'pink-collar ghettos'. When you combine low status with hierarchy, it is clear that many of these societies lack the open and safe environment needed for women to speak up.

I once interviewed for a job with an Italian company. After several positive interviews, I asked the head of HR for some time to discuss the opportunity with my wife. His friendly attitude immediately disappeared and—with a look hovering between pity and disgust—he walked me out. Three days later I got a call from somebody on his team telling me they had decided to look for another candidate. They felt I was not a good cultural fit. After getting over the rejection, both my wife and I agreed it was for the best.

Power Distance

Power distance is the degree to which members of a group expect and accept power to be distributed equally.

- In low power distance societies like The Netherlands, Sweden and Australia, the ideal degree of separation between a boss and subordinates is relatively low. The supervisor is a facilitator among equals and organisational structures are flat, so that communication can skip hierarchical bounds. Feedback is a more interactive process (e.g. 360-degree assessments) that reaches a deeper level of information. Asking for feedback is accepted and even encouraged. Individuals will seek feedback from subordinates and superiors more than they will their peers.

- In high power distance cultures like Morocco, Russia and Spain, the ideal distance between bosses and subordinates is high. The boss is a strong director and the decision maker, leading from the front, without the need to consult with followers. Members are not expected to disagree. Organisational structures are multi-layered and fixed and communication travels down the hierarchy in that feedback is given from the top down. Individuals look for personal feedback from their peers more than they do their bosses or subordinates.

Having been a part of several multicultural teams, both as a leader and as a member, I have seen different attitudes to hierarchy provoking immense frustration in both high and low power distance colleagues. The more hierarchical teammates complain that others do not respect authority and they take on decisions that are not theirs to make. The low power distance team members complain that more hierarchical team members hold everything up—incapable of doing anything without feedback and approval from their supervisors. This situation slows projects down and demotivates the team.

Cultural Origins Predict Death in Mountains

A study by Columbia and INSEAD Business School of 30,625 Himalayan mountain climbers from 56 countries on 5,104 expeditions found that climbers from hierarchical countries had more climbers in groups reach the summit, but also had more climbers die along the way.[24] Hierarchy helps groups perform well by clearly defining roles, facilitating coordination and avoiding conflict, especially in stable and well-defined environments. However, rigid hierarchy discourages lower-ranked climbers from speaking up and identifying critical errors or safety concerns. In rapidly changing and extreme conditions like the Himalayas you need the perspective of all the team members to return to base. It is on the way down that most climbers die as extreme fatigue, blurred thinking and harsh conditions take their biggest toll. The findings also showed that cultural values could predict behaviour even if people are far from home, especially when faced with uncertainty.

Personality and Feedback

Personality refers to individual differences in the way we think, feel and behave. These traits have two genetic components: the *nature* component and the *nurture* component. The degree to which traits are influenced by our genes versus our childhood experiences is still a matter of debate, but it is safe to say that a caring, secure childhood gives a person a great start in life.

Numerous methodologies and models exist for mapping personality. They are widely used in organisations and offer a useful starting point for understanding.

The Five-Factor Model (also known as the BIG Five or the OCEAN/CANOE) is considered one of the most reliable and academically validated models in the world, using dimensions along which all people can be placed, with the majority of people falling in the middle categories.[25] The dimensions are: Openness, Conscientiousness, Extraversion, Agreeableness and Neuroticism.

Personality Problems

On a sunny day in June 1994, an Air Force Boeing B-52 Stratofortress crashed at Fairchild Air Force Base in the United States, while practising for a demonstration flight at an air show later that year. Behind the controls was Lt. Col. Arthur 'Bud' Holland, who, after a few low passes over the airfield, flew the bomber in a tight left turn around the control tower, where the aircraft stalled beyond control. The B52 bomber crashed, killing Holland and three other crewmembers on board. The crash was captured on video and the sad images were repeatedly shown in the media around the world.

The accident investigation concluded that amongst other factors, Holland's personality and reckless behaviour played a significant role in the sequence of events that led to the crash. Air Force personnel testified that Holland had a reputation as an aggressive pilot who often broke flight safety and other rules. When confronted with his behaviour by (junior) fellow crewmembers, Holland—on several occasions—laughed them away and called his colleagues 'Pussies'. Some Air Force colleagues refused to fly with Holland.

Here's a quick breakdown of these big five personality traits:

1. Openness to Experience

Are you inventive and curious, or consistent and cautious?

Openness reflects the depth of your intellectual curiosity, creativity and preference for novelty and variety over a strict routine. It describes the extent to which you are imaginative and independent.

Those of us with a high level of openness to new experiences are more open to receiving feedback than people who are more routine-based.

2. Conscientiousness

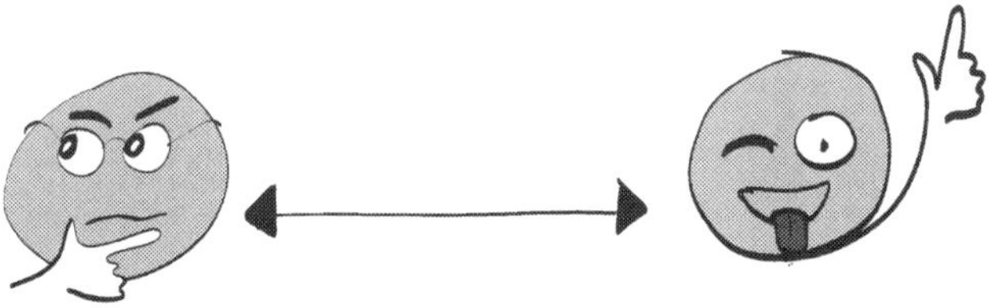

Are you efficient and organised, or easy-going and carefree?

Conscientiousness relates to whether you prefer planned versus spontaneous behaviour and reveals your tendency toward being dependable, showing self-discipline, acting dutifully and aiming for achievement.

Once conscientious people know it's part of their job, they are more likely to provide feedback; they'll see it as another task to be performed dutifully.

3. Extraversion

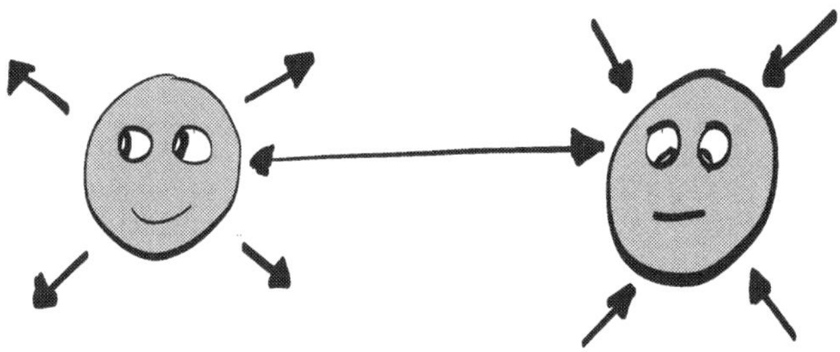

Are you outgoing and energetic, or solitary and reserved? Extraversion is revealed by your energy, talkativeness, positive emotions, assertiveness, sociability and the tendency to seek stimulation in the company of others.

While receiving feedback, extroverted people are more likely to consider the positive and block out the negative. They also regularly ask clarifying questions and focus on maintaining good relationships.

4. Agreeableness

Are you friendly and compassionate, or analytical and detached?

Agreeableness is measured by your tendency to be compassionate, empathetic and cooperative rather than suspicious and antagonistic towards others.

With their compassionate and empathetic natures, highly agreeable people are more likely to build strong and trusting relationships. They tend to begin the feedback process on a positive note, making it easier to deliver messages in a constructive way. They also tend to maintain positive impressions of others, which makes them more likely to accept others' intentions at face value during a feedback session.

5. Neuroticism

Are you sensitive and nervous, or secure and confident?

Neurotic people experience unpleasant emotions easily, including anger, anxiety, depression and chronic stress. Neuroticism describes your degree of emotional stability, self-confidence and impulse control.

Extremely neurotic people, due to their sensitive and insecure nature, will almost certainly feel threatened and experience negative emotions while receiving feedback.

Individuals with higher self-esteem accept positive feedback more readily because it is consistent with their expectations and self-image. They are less disturbed by negative feedback because their high level of self-compassion cushions the impact.

With any personality test, it is important to keep in mind that humans are too complex to classify into simple types or dimensions. Moreover, as we grow, we change. Personality development is the lifelong process of managing all the part of ourselves—moving from ignorance to competence.

Generations and Feedback

Different generations view—and value—feedback in various ways. In general people often mistakenly think that high experience levels and seniority eliminate the need for further learning and therefore feedback.

- Baby Boomers, the oldest remaining generation in the workplace, tend to see feedback as an assessment of performance; a yearly event where you are judged and receive either a bonus or a penalty. This is by no means something you would want every day.
- Generation X operates in the same way, but the prize is not necessarily money; it can also be freedom and empowerment.
- Generations Y, or Millennials, live in a world of social networking, where asking for and receiving feedback, immediately, is a part of everyday life. You post a question, a picture or a comment

and you expect—and often receive—immediate feedback. Because this generation is so used to getting results at the touch of a button, they also require more feedback than any other generation. They see feedback in the workplace as a quick way to learn from personal interactions in an 'on-demand' way, which means that they do not often take things personally or feel judged. Millennials genuinely crave tips, suggestions and coaching to improve themselves and get ready for their next position, inside or outside of the company. They are easily bored and as such, loyalty is to people and projects rather than to the organisation.

- Generation Z, the most formally educated generation and the most technology switched on generation, will have the same feedback expectations as the Millennials, as they enter the workforce over the next years.

Tips for Dealing with the Feedback Generation:

- Acknowledge Millennials' contributions regularly, or correct them immediately if they ought to do something different. In the absence of feedback, millennials typically assume everything is okay.

- Just because they crave feedback does not mean they know how to give it. Social media feedback is fast, simplistic and 'like for like'—not always the type of feedback appropriate for the workplace. All generations need to become more skilful at feedback.

Gender and Feedback

As we explored in our earlier discussion about culture, male assertiveness and motherly care are universal stereotypic portraits, even in highly egalitarian societies. Studies show that men are seen as more strong, aggressive and proactive, whereas women are considered more communal, expressive, gentle and passive than men.[26] These stereotypes naturally show up at work, where at least two research studies have found that men and women are given significantly different feedback at work, regardless of whether the manager delivering the feedback is male or female.[27] For example, women are more likely to receive vague feedback when it comes to their achievements, good or bad. It seems that men are offered a clearer picture of what they are doing well and more specific guidance as to what is needed to get to the next level.

On the other hand, women are 2.5 times more likely to get specific critical feedback about an aggressive communication style; a form of expression that is encouraged in men. When women show leadership behaviours such as assertiveness and decisiveness, they tend to be seen as competent but not personable or sympathetic. Those who do adopt a more stereotypically feminine style are liked more, but not seen as strong leaders: a no-win situation.

The Takeaways

- Our mental software is made up of human nature, culture and personality. By being aware of the impact of these three programs we are better prepared to give and receive feedback.
- The influence of human nature on feedback can be understood by looking at four basic universal drives:

    a. The drive to achieve.
    b. The drive to bond.
    c. The drive to learn.
    d. The drive to defend.

- Human biases and stereotypes distort reality, usually in our favour.
- The words used for feedback can easily trigger defensiveness resulting in aggression, withdrawal or subtler—often unconscious—ways of protecting our self-esteem.
- National culture subconsciously affects the way we think, feel and act at home and in the office. The GLOBE research programme shows that assertiveness, collectivism, gender egalitarianism and power distance influence feedback behaviour.

- The OCEAN personality model offers a good starting point to explore the link between feedback and Openness, Consciousness, Extraversion, Agreeableness and Neuroticism.

- The younger generations in the workplace today expect feedback to learn and advance fast.

- Universal gender stereotypes and biases make it difficult for women to speak up and fully participate in professional life.

- If we combine the effects of our mental software, we can distinguish 5 behaviours that form barriers to productive feedback:
    a. Staying silent.
    b. Confusing opinions with facts.
    c. Choosing the wrong words.
    d. Holding on to inflated self-views.
    e. Defensiveness.

PART II: THE CLEAR+CALM MODEL

2

INTRODUCTION TO CLEAR+CALM FEEDBACK

Courage is what it takes to stand up and speak; courage is also what it takes to sit down and listen.

Sir Winston Churchill

IN AN INCREASINGLY dynamic and global world, the capacity to provide and absorb feedback effectively is essential, especially if you want to make optimal use of all the brainpower you've worked so hard to recruit: let's call it our collective intelligence. This may sound obvious, but we've all seen poorly prepared, timed and received feedback cause damage to egos, relationships and performance.

The CLEAR+CALM model has been created to manage feedback from the giver and receiver point of view. We have used insights from neuroscience, psychology, culture and teamwork, especially Crew Resource Management in aviation. The model provides a common approach to feedback and gives clear guidelines for behaviour that works and that doesn't work; we learn from both.

Here's what the letters in CLEAR and CALM stand for:

CLEAR Steps:

- **C**onstructive: Prepare the case.
- **L**anguage: Words matter.
- **E**valuate: Manage reactions.
- **A**ction: Reach an agreement.
- **R**elationship: Move on.

CALM Steps:

- **C**onsider: Put yourself in the shoes of the giver.
- **A**wareness: Know yourself.
- **L**isten: Control Yourself.
- **M**anage: Actively question.

Depending on the circumstances and the feedback skills of both giver and receiver, some steps of the model can be more relevant than others. In chapters 5, 6 and 7 we will focus specifically on using CLEAR+CALM for feedback under pressure, positive feedback and asking for feedback.

It is All About Behaviour

The model provides the awareness and the critical moves to navigate feedback across cultures and hierarchies. Here are two essential preliminary steps:

1. **Develop Situational Awareness**. In chapter 1 we discussed the theory of feedback through different lenses like culture or personality. Understanding these dynamics is essential to improving. Low situational awareness of what is going on around, and inside, you can be dangerous.

2. **Understand the Critical Moves.** We have tried to be as specific as possible when describing the behaviours needed for giving and receiving feedback; you either do them or you don't. A lot of change initiatives fail because the new behaviour is not clearly defined. Organisations want to become more agile or collaborative, but nobody knows what that actually looks like.

Who Benefits?

The CLEAR+CALM model works for three—overlapping—groups of users:

- **Individuals**—leaders and followers—who want to improve their communication and influencing skills, both on the giving and the receiving side.
- **Individual teams or parts of the organisation** who want to use feedback to improve their performance, despite the conflicting cultural norms inside or outside their organisation.
- **Organisations** that want to build feedback into the corporate culture to serve as a buffer against the personal preferences or cultural norms that slow down open and honest communication. Building a feedback culture greatly helps individuals and teams achieve their feedback goals!

Preparing the Foundations for a Feedback Culture

The real magic happens when the entire organisation adopts the principles of CLEAR+CALM. Full participation really helps to overcome the conflict and fear that feedback can produce.

There are many different types of organisational culture. In some cultures, feedback is the norm, but in others it is avoided. The way power is distributed—by person, position, or task—impacts feedback practice. The more rigid the hierarchy the more difficult it is to challenge authority.

We often compare a feedback culture with a basecamp for climbers. Basecamp is a place where everybody comes together to set the norms, practice skills and build strong relationships before setting out to reach the summit. Climbers feel safe knowing that when they ask questions they will not be ridiculed, punished or ignored. When it is time to climb, speaking up and listening continues to be the norm, even in extreme conditions. Basecamp culture has prepared the team for top performance. Without it, climbers would face a dangerous and deadly journey to the top.

It is the same in organisations: if we feel safe, well trained and confident we use feedback to reach our own 'summit' goals.

Tips for Building a Feedback Infrastructure:

- Top management can greatly speed up the introduction and long-term success by publicly endorsing and role modelling CLEAR+CALM feedback behaviours: this is the way we do it.
- Avoid flashy communication campaigns without visible and real management support. Vague words and empty promises provoke cynicism and demotivation.
- Continuously train everybody in giving and receiving feedback to improve skills and develop confidence.
- Recognise good feedback behaviour and immediately correct bad feedback behaviour.
- Train managers and hold them responsible for providing a safe environment for people to speak up. We will discuss safe feedback environments in chapter 9 of the book.

Feedback across Borders

Effective feedback in a homogeneous culture can often prove quite challenging; diverse feedback norms and styles in multicultural environments make feedback even more complex.

Tips for Promoting Feedback in Multicultural Environments:

1. Agree on a corporate language, that everyone speaks (English, Spanish, etc.). We have the tendency to flip back to our mother tongue when we are with compatriots, effectively shutting out other colleagues.
2. Before learning about other cultures, understand your own cultural feedback style.
3. Explain and make fun of your own culture to increase understanding and lower status and threat. Of course, in some cultures, this is not always possible. I usually start all my trainings and presentations with a: 'I apologize in advance for my brutally Dutch directness… it's nothing personal'.
4. Be careful with humour, cynicism and sarcasm.
5. At a minimum, study and compare the feedback styles of the cultures you move around in. Remember that companies and their leaders reflect their national cultures (Go to: **futureteaming.com/culture-feedback-tool** for more information).

The Takeaways

- The CLEAR+CALM model provides the guidelines and behaviours for giving and receiving feedback across cultures and hierarchies.
- A clear understanding of the human dynamics of feedback is key to using the model.
- The model clearly describes the behaviour needed for feedback. Therefore, you can train, asses and discuss CLEAR+CALM steps.
- The CLEAR+CALM model can be used for different types of feedback: giving, receiving, emergency feedback, positive feedback and asking for feedback.
- The CLEAR+CALM steps work for individuals, teams and organisations.
- To build a feedback culture, leaders needs to get involved and role model.
- In international organisations the common feedback language, like CLEAR+CALM, can connect different cultures and buffer against norms that hinder feedback.

3

CLEAR STEPS FOR GIVING EFFECTIVE FEEDBACK

Our lives begin to end the day we become silent about things that matter.

Martin Luther King Jr.

THE CLEAR PART of our model provides guidelines for giving effective feedback. It focuses on the facts while nurturing the relationship. Let's call it the *carefrontational* approach: confronting facts in a caring manner! It's not easy, but small improvements can make a big difference. If the receiver is listening and learning, that means your feedback was appropriate and skilful. If he or she seems to be in denial, defensive, or failing to make progress, you need to improve your approach.

Let's have a look at the CLEAR model for giving

skilful feedback. Here's how it works, using our acronym CLEAR:

- **C**onstructive: Prepare the case.
- **L**anguage: Words matter.
- **E**valuate: Manage reactions.
- **A**ction: Reach an agreement.
- **R**elationship: Move on.

And here are the steps.

Step 1: Constructive – Prepare the Case –

The first step of CLEAR is all about preparation. Before you give feedback you should explore the why, what, how, when and where of feedback.

Depending on the circumstances and the urgency of the situation, not all questions need to be answered. The general rule is the bigger the impact, the more preparation you need.

I often write a feedback 'script' and review my notes at least once to separate the facts from assumptions or interpretations. Then I practice it with a neutral observer, who can point out potential problems and improvements. Arguments may flow wonderfully in my mind, but they do not always come across as such in person—especially if I have to speak a foreign language.

1.1 Be Clear About the Purpose of Feedback

The purpose of giving feedback is to improve a specific behaviour for the better. If you set out to change the person instead, you are more likely to provoke defensiveness and resistance.

Questions to Consider Before Giving Feedback:

1. What behaviour is the problem and what is the negative impact on me, the team, the company and the world?
2. Should the receiver take the feedback as friendly advice, an invitation for discussion, or an order with consequences for disobeying?
3. Am I giving the person feedback with the intention

to help them grow and make a positive difference or am I just showing power or dumping frustration?

4. Is feedback the best way to address the issue, or are there other ways to solve the problem? I am chaotic by nature. But intensive feedback sessions with bosses and team members have helped me become more organised. The biggest improvement came when my manager told me to accept my weaknesses and get support from others. I now make sure I always work together with orderly colleagues, who have helped me double my productivity and my engagement.

1.2 Choose The Right Time and Place for Feedback

It's important to give feedback as soon as possible, so the events leading up to the conversation are still fresh in people's minds. In addition, the faster mistakes or opportunities are addressed, the quicker performance goes up. This is the essence of agility! Making a long list for discussion at the annual performance review is, therefore, a bad idea. By then, the facts and the circumstances may not be so clear. Suppressing feedback for too long can also lead to a situation in which all your pent-up frustration suddenly pours out, often at the worst possible moment.

However, if you feel offended, angry or sad, it is better to delay the feedback until you can regain perspective and empathise with the receiver. Your brain can become emotionally flooded and shut down rational reasoning, which is precisely the kind of thinking you need for learning conversations.

Timing also needs to match the company culture and work environment. Some organisations can deal with ad-hoc and unplanned feedback; others might call for scheduling the feedback meeting or making it part of a weekly meeting. There is no right or wrong way of doing this as long as you have an opportunity bring up the issue as soon as possible.

Tips for Timing Feedback:

1. Ask the receiver for a convenient time to talk. This shows respect and gives her some sense of control. Walking in on a colleague who is busy, stressed or preoccupied will not get you off to a good start.
2. Do not give 'hit-and-run' feedback, hoping the receiver will take it all in and make the change.
3. Select a quiet, private place where you are not likely to be interrupted by anyone or anything. In general, nobody wants to receive negative feed-back when other people are around, especially in cultures where losing face in front of the group is a highly stressful experience.
4. Give feedback in person if possible. The more likely it is that the feedback will emotionally impact the receiver, the more important it is to be in the same room. Telephone conversations and discussions over social media can be confusing. These channels do not transmit body language, which is an important part of communication.

1.3 Take into Account the Position of the Receiver

Try to imagine the world from the receiver's perspective, regardless of how his or her views differ from your own. We are more likely to change our attitudes and behaviours when we feel heard, understood and respected. The more you know about the receiver—including his or her personality, rank and culture—the more you can give feedback that resonates and the more you can anticipate the receiver's reaction. In aviation, this is called 'situational awareness':, or simply knowing what is going on around you.

Step 2: Language
- Words Matter -

Once you have prepared your feedback, it is important to find the right language to give it in.

2.1 Use Positive Language

Feedback can easily be interpreted as dislike, disrespect, or a lack of love, threatening our relationships with others. This is why it is smart to start a feedback session with some general appreciation for the receiver. Starting with positive reinforcement will calm emotions, delay defensive reactions and motivate the receiver to continue improving, as long as your words are genuine and carefully formulated. If the receiver assumes that you're only giving positive feedback as a means of softening the negative feedback, something is obviously not working.

The best ratio of positive reinforcement to negative comments is difficult to determine. However, to be on the safe side, positive feedback should outnumber negative feedback by 5:1. In 1990, Harvard psychology professor John Gottman researched married couples and found that marriages were considerably more stable if there were five times as many positive feelings and interactions between the spouses as there were negative ones.[28] Gottman called this the 'magic ratio'.

Tips for Showing Genuine Appreciation and Gratitude:

1. Assure the receiver that he or she is a valued colleague and member of the team.
2. Tell the receiver that you think he or she has the potential to improve.
3. Stress that the feedback is not about dislike or bringing up problems for the sake of bringing up problems. Feedback is about learning and getting better.

4. Avoid using the word 'but' as it immediately diminishes the positive recognition and primes people to focus on the negative ('You are one of our best project managers, but your presentation was weak').

2.2 Use Direct and Action-Focused Statements

Direct, clear and respectful language promotes straightforward and honest conversations that enable quick learning and change. Providing negative feedback in vague or abstract terms might avoid conflict, but it slows everything down or may even go unnoticed. When you give feedback in an ambiguous manner, people are left confused and uncertain about what is expected of them. Dubious communication can also be interpreted as untrue and therefore unfair. If we feel we are being treated unfairly, defensiveness is likely to follow.

Tips for Giving Direct Feedback:

1. Avoid acting hurt or disappointed.
2. Do not shut people out or avoid them.

3. Beware of body language. A big part of human communication is non-verbal. Keep an open and friendly posture.
4. Do not ask leading questions that push toward a particular answer ('Don't you think your presentation was unprofessional?').
5. Avoid sarcasm by saying the opposite of your real opinion. ('Thank you so much for being on time, we are really happy you found some time to join us…NOT').

2.3 Use Relevant Facts

As we know by now, good feedback is built on facts, not assumptions. When we are calm, we usually take the time to do our homework and come up with well-founded arguments. When we are stressed, we are more likely to take shortcuts and jump to conclusions. In today's world, we are often busy, with limited time and attention to interpret our surroundings. As such, we often settle on the first acceptable—but biased—explanation. Remember we see the world through rose-coloured glasses and our memories are anything but reliable, 'photographic', records of events.

Tips for Sticking to the Facts:

1. Use fact-based language and avoid sweeping statements about the receiver's personality or character.
2. Focus on describing the problematic behaviour(s), but realise that your perceptions may only be part of the story. Be ready to hear the other side.
3. Give clear examples and illustrations of the facts and behaviours.
4. Avoid using amplifying words like 'absolutely', 'totally', 'strongly' and 'actually' to describe the negative behaviours.
5. When in doubt, use words or phrases that can soften the cold hard facts, such as 'kind of', 'sort of', 'a bit' and 'slightly'.
6. Avoid using sweeping generalisations when describing behaviours. Words like 'always', 'typically' and 'never' imply a character problem.
7. Say 'I' not 'we' when you are talking about your own experience or perception. 'When you arrived late, we were all disappointed' vs. 'When you came late, I was disappointed'. Although the argument might sound stronger by generalising the experience, it can provoke a defensive and paranoid, 'Who is we?!' response.

Step 3: Evaluate
- Manage Reactions -

3.1 Listen Calmly

It's crucial to stay calm and listen when the receiver reacts or responds to your feedback. New information might change your view. Listening also has a calming effect on the receiver as it signals interest, respect and care.

To avoid the 'so what?' reaction, it may be necessary to reemphasize the negative impact of business outcomes. Remember that merely pointing out the behaviour might not be enough to change it.

Tips for Listening:

1. Ask open-ended questions to understand the receiver's point of view. Changes in attitude and behaviour are more likely to occur when the receiver feels understood, heard and respected.
2. Listen actively, resisting the temptation to jump

to conclusions or come up with smart answers while the receiver is still talking.

3. Summarise, paraphrase and repeat words back to the receiver to demonstrate you are truly listening. Start your sentence by opening with: 'Let me check if I have understood you well' or 'Let me summarise what I just heard you say'.
4. Take a time-out if your emotions are about to trigger anger and conflict, especially in a multi-cultural setting.

3.2 Give the Benefit of the Doubt

We can be somewhat paranoid when it comes to predicting the intentions of others, especially if we feel disappointed or threatened. Although it's possible that behaviour is selfish, corrupt or evil, that happens far less often than people think. We tend to do things for many different reasons, some of which we don't even understand ourselves. Therefore, it is better to focus on facts, not conspiracy theories. Always try to give people the benefit of the doubt; they probably did not mean to do harm.

3.3 Understand Your Contribution to the Problem

Often, problematic behaviour can be traced back to the way we work with people. Without realising it, we may have become part of a 'system' in which our actions trigger reactions in others. To us, it seems obvious who is to blame. So, it is important to figure out if you are somehow part of the problem—and, as such, whether you are responsible for part of the solution. If the receiver does not volunteer any information on the matter, it's best to simply ask. This also shows that you do not feel perfect or superior. Feedback, after all, is a learning conversation for both the giver and the receiver.

Step 4: Action
- Reach an Agreement -

4.1 Focus on a Desired Future

Dwelling on the past or focusing on what is wrong creates defensiveness and resistance. We may feel stuck with a failed past, but we can do something about creating a better future. When you frame feedback as a means of reaching a positive goal for the future, it becomes an opportunity to solve a business problem rather than a personal one. Feedback becomes feedforward.

Tips for Feedforward:

1. Do not humiliate the receiver by making her relive her mistakes—most people tend to be hard enough on themselves as it is.
2. Give the receiver ideas on how he can become even better. By choosing between different options he maintains a feeling of control.

3. Use the observed behaviour that led to problems in the past to build a desirable scenario for the future. 'How can we make sure you are on time for the next meeting' vs. 'You were late again. Do you know how annoying this is?'.

4.2 Involve the Receiver

The more the receiver feels involved and motivated to come up with his own solutions, the more he is likely to take responsibility and make positive changes. For a meaningful agreement about change be ready to compromise. Examples: If Tom agrees to stop using his mobile during meetings you could promise to keep them short and to the point. If Miki keeps her presentation shorter the rest of the team will pay attention and ask more questions.

4.3 Brainstorm SMART Goals

Once both the giver and the receiver have agreed on a possible solution, it is important to break it down into clear, non-negotiable behaviours: things you can either do or not do. Vague terms might come across as more professional in the short-term, but they will lead to differences in interpretation and confusion in the long run: 'You need to be more agile!' can mean different things to different people. The SMART filter can help translate goals into behaviours that can be followed up.

SMART Questions to Clarify:

Specific: What are the exact behaviours or activities we have to stop or start?

Measurable: How can we measure if it works?

Assignable: Who is responsible for starting or stopping the behaviours?

Realistic: Are the behaviours or actions we have agreed on realistic?

Time-related: When will these behaviours stop or start?

In my previous example: 'You need to be more agile' should be translated into a mutually agreed goal: 'I will respond to emails from customers within 2 working days, starting next Monday.'

Changes in mind-set and attitude don't necessarily translate into changes in behaviour. Once the giver and the receiver have agreed on common goals, they must follow up with each other regularly to make sure new behaviour turns into lasting habits.

Step 5: Relationship
- Move on -

5.1 Re-establish the Relationship

Even if the feedback was delivered clearly and received calmly, it is important to spend some time strengthening the relationship once the discussion is over. Going back to the magic ratio of positive and negative interactions for successful relationships, Gottman's research showed that it wasn't only how couples communicated that mattered, but also how they made up after a conflict.

It is essential to make the receiver feel positive and safe, not guilty or humiliated. People may appear calm and yet they still feel frustrated, hurt or ashamed on the inside; we are all a bit paranoid and tend to fixate on the negative. Wounds to our self-esteem heal faster in an environment where mistakes are seen as incentives to improve.

5.2 Offer a Fresh Start

To move on, it is important that the receiver feels that the matter has been resolved and closed. If the receiver suspects you are keeping a—real or mental—blacklist of mistakes, paranoia and doom can take over. The thought that your reputation or relationships are permanently damaged can be demotivating.

Tips for Normalising and Balancing the Relationship:

1. At the end of the feedback session, add a normalising remark that shows nothing has changed: you still trust and value the receiver and his work. ('Tina, thanks for the discussion! You are one of our best sales people and we cannot hit our targets without you.').
2. Explain that mistakes are learning opportunities for everyone. ('We have all learned from this experience, now, let's move on and make it work.').
3. Make some unrelated and more personal remarks to show you still value her friendship and company. ('About the barbecue tomorrow; shall I bring the hamburgers?').

5.3 Ask for Feedback on Feedback

Another effective and courageous way to restore balance to the relationship is to ask the receiver to give feedback on your feedback. This shows humility and acknowledges the fact that you do not consider yourself superior or smarter: it restores the power balance.

It also signals that you, too, are keen to learn and improve yourself, which may encourage the receiver to do the same.

The Takeaways

1. **Constructive: Prepare the case**
   1. Be clear about the purpose of the feedback.
   2. Choose the right time and place for feedback.
   3. Take into account the position of the receiver.
2. **Language: Words Matter**
   1. Use positive language.
   2. Use direct and action-focused statements.
   3. Use relevant facts.
3. **Evaluate: Manage Reactions**
   1. Listen calmly.
   2. Give the benefit of the doubt.
   3. Understand your contribution to the problem.
4. **Action: Reach an Agreement**
   1. Focus on a desired future.
   2. Involve the receiver.
   3. Brainstorm SMART goals.
5. **Relationship: We move on**
   1. Re-establish the relationship.
   2. Offer a fresh start.
   3. Ask for feedback on feedback.

4

CALM STEPS FOR RECEIVING FEEDBACK PRODUCTIVELY

If I try to insult you about something you don't buy into, it will just roll off your back. The only insults that hurt are the ones you buy into.

Gervase R. Bushe

WHEN WE ARE on the receiving end of feedback, we often assume that it is our role is to accept and react. However, a skilled receiver can take the initiative and offer an agenda. Dealing effectively with feedback is as important as giving good feedback, which almost never happens—at least not perfectly. If the feedback is not clear, or if it seems unfair, we must ask for clarification. By managing any defensive reactions and showing empathy, the idea of being talked *to* can be turned into talking *with*.

The CALM part of the CLEAR+CALM model shows you how to deal with feedback in the best way possible: stay calm and curious. Here's how it works, using our acronym CALM.

- **C**onsider: Put yourself in the shoes of the giver.
- **A**wareness: Know yourself.
- **L**isten: Control yourself.
- **M**anage: Actively question.

And here are the steps.

Step 1: Consider
- Put Yourself in the Shoes of the Giver -

1.1 Show Empathy

It's important to control immediate impulses to defend yourself so you have time to explore the perspective of the giver: Where is she coming from and what is her story? Tune into what the giver might be thinking and feeling about the situation, regardless of how that view might differ from your perception.

Questions to explore the state of mind:

1. Does the giver seem to be in an emotional mood or stressed; could there be something else going on?
2. Is the giver sensitive to certain triggers: topics, values, behaviours, biases, etc.?

3. Are there any cultural differences that may play a role in the situation?

1.2 Unpack Feedback for Deeper Meaning

It's important to look beyond literal language for deeper meaning. Even if the feedback may seem a bit awkward, disrespectful, or insensitive, it does not mean the underlying message is wrong, inaccurate, or politically motivated. Few people have been trained to give feedback and so it can provoke serious tension; nobody likes to be seen as cruel, disrespectful, or hypocritical. It is important that we give feedback the benefit of the doubt, even if it is not immediately clear whether it is valid or useful. Learning conversations can develop, even after a false start.

Tips for Exploring Feedback:

1. Resist the temptation to (mis)use insensitive feedback to reject the feedback you've received.
2. Ask yourself if the feedback—or part of it—is fair, even if the words came out wrong.

3. Don't neutralise poorly delivered feedback with positive comments from other sources (e.g. 'You tell me I am a negative person, but other people assure me I am an enthusiastic colleague').

1.3 Separate the Message from the Messenger

It's important to isolate your opinions about the giver from the message he is delivering. Even if he is not the most credible, trusted, or experienced person to give the feedback, there still may be truth in the message. This separation is not as easy as it sounds, as we are hyper-sensitive to other people's intentions: motives matter. The bigger the negative impact, the more you may feel attacked and assume that the giver is trying to hurt you on purpose. Feedback that comes from a genuine attempt to help is easier to accept than criticism driven by power games or cruelty.

Step 2. Awareness
- Know Yourself -

2.1. Recognize Your Emotions

If you can recognise and 'sit with' your emotions, you can catch yourself before striking back. An immediate attack on the giver can often spiral into a full-scale battle, which can destroy relationships. On the other hand, giving in without fully understanding or accepting the feedback is not productive either; you don't learn anything and you are left feeling hurt and humiliated.

Tips to Understanding Emotions:

1. Take a time-out to think. Being mindful of your

emotions and feelings as they come up gives you more control over your behaviour.

2. Name the emotion. If you know why you feel anxious you can manage the emotion. Are you angry, ashamed, disgusted or afraid?
3. Remember the difference between human and monkey thinking—Are you trying to understand the situation or acting on defensive impulses?

2.2 Be Aware How You Tend to Deal with Feedback

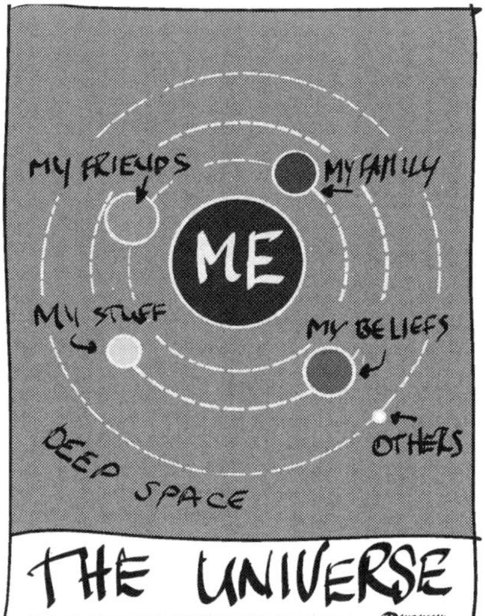

First of all, remember that we frequently see the world through rose-coloured glasses. We're often overoptimistic about our own capabilities, but quick to make negative assumptions about others. When we give feedback, we notice the receiver is not good at accepting it. When we receive feedback, we observe the giver isn't good at delivering it. So, if we all think we are a bit better than we really are, it is clear that feedback can easily come across as inaccurate or unfair.

It is vital, therefore, to understand how you tend to deal with feedback.

Questions for Self-reflection:

1. Am I usually sensitive and insecure when receiving feedback or are there specific topics which make it worse?
2. Do I have certain 'shame buttons'[29]: images I carry of myself as not being good enough? For example, a remark about a mistake can push the 'I am not smart enough' button. This can make you defend yourself against your own judgement, rather than what the other person said or did.
3. How fast do I recuperate my sense of self-esteem and optimism?
4. Can I live with the short-term discomfort that feedback provides, in exchange for long-term learning?

2.3 Understand how Others Perceive You

When it comes to understanding how others see us, it's important not to stay in the dark. Lack of self-awareness—personal tendencies, cultural norms, values, beliefs, etc.—can seriously undermine your credibility; blissful ignorance is seen as immature in all cultures. Receiving feedback and using this information to adjust the view you have of yourself is key for personal and professional growth. I sometimes ask a team member to observe me in important meetings or presentations. They have confirmed that I have a tendency to move too fast and not take enough time to explain my thinking. It is so obvious to me what needs to be done that if I am not stopped I will assume everybody is on board: I have a naïve view of reality.

My team and I came up with three improvements I still use to this day. Firstly, I force myself to give more background information. Secondly, I asked my team to clearly signal when I am going too fast. Thirdly, I ask them to summarise what they have just heard me say. I do my part and my team helps me stay on track: we share responsibility.

If self-awareness is so important, then why do so many people lack it? One reason is that most people refrain from giving each other feedback out of politeness or discomfort. To gain influence and protect our relationships, we tell white lies. If you have always received positive feedback, accepting negative feedback can be difficult. We start to believe the hype, even if the evidence is against us. Remember the notion of confirmation bias; once we believe in something, we will go out of our way to find the evidence to support it.

To make things worse, by nature we are not good at understanding how others see us: 'I think I'm a good, effective, talented person...and so others must see me that way, too'. This 'self-serving bias' amplifies the good and blocks out the bad, enhancing our self-esteem and giving us a positive outlook on life. The dark side of this 'productive narcissism' is that it makes it difficult to see that we might be wrong and need to improve.

Tips for Understanding Your Public Image:

1. Regularly ask for feedback after completing a project or task. The more you do it the easier it gets.
2. Do a 360-degree assessment, where you ask supervisors, peers, subordinates and even family and friends about how they see you in areas like leadership or emotional intelligence. Every group will look at you from a different perspective. Compare the results with your own view to see if there are any gaps or blind spots.
3. Get a coach. A person who is trained to ask questions and hold up a mirror is a gift. Because coaches are neutral experts, you likely will find it easier to open up, accept reality and still feel safe. A 'carefrontational' approach can break through defences and provide confidence to improve.

Step 3: Listen
- Control Yourself -

3.1 Show Confidence

When you can control your impulse to become defensive in the face of upsetting feedback—even if it's only at some crucial moments—it gives you valuable time to determine the next move. Moreover, it signals to the giver that you are taking them seriously. Listening and reflecting on the feedback calms the giver, which is important, as feedback can provoke lots of anxiety. Take a time-out if you feel your emotions are about to trigger anger or conflict, especially in a multi-cultural setting. Displaying intense negative emotions is regarded differently across cultures.

Tips to Show Confidence:

1. Calmly take notes. Writing down the feedback shows you are calm and listening.
2. Nod and make small sounds of understanding ('yes', 'ok', 'I understand').

3. Speak slowly in a relaxed tone of voice. If you feel your throat or facial muscles tensing, try to relax them.

3.2 Control the Impulse to Act

Accept feelings, control actions. How you express feelings like fear and anger is up to you; attack back, run for cover, or remain calm. When you allow emotions to hijack your mind it is impossible to think straight and learn. You have an angry monkey jumping around in your head and if you let it out, somebody will get hurt. The oldest part of our brain, often called 'Reptilian', is hardwired to protect us from danger. This defence system kept us safe from sabre-toothed tigers 10,000 years ago and it still rules our behaviour today, often inappropriately.

Tips for Controlling Impulses:

1. Be aware of paranoid, suspicious and fatalistic thoughts, which indicate that your brain is in 'monkey mode'.
2. 'Park' your thoughts and impulses to act; you can always come back to them later, instead of pretending they are not there. For example, if you feel offended by feedback, quickly write down what you would like to say or do. Later, once you fully understand the situation, read back your notes to see if your responses still make sense. Much of the time, you will be happy you did not turn thought into action.
3. Blow off steam if you get too excited, but do it with a trusted friend or colleague—NOT with the feedback giver. The crucial point is to get frustration off your chest so you can think things through clearly.

3.3 Stay Open to New Information

Highly emotional discussions are difficult to manage and usually lead to a state of emotional flooding, a state where the brain can no longer process information in a rational and productive manner. We lose our capacity to listen and be empathetic. To avoid conflict, it is important the giver can tell his full story.

Tips for Remaining Open:

1. **Keep a friendly expression**. A relaxed and interested appearance will calm the giver.
2. **Watch your body language**. Keep eye contact, lean forward and don't cross your arms.
3. **Let the giver talk**. Do not interrupt or finish sentences for the giver.

Step 4: Manage
- Actively Question -

4.1 Use the CLEAR Steps for Clarification

If you think the giver might have some misconceptions about you, but that she also may also have some helpful comments, you can encourage her to provide more actionable feedback using the CLEAR steps. Ask open-ended questions and listen actively, resisting the temptation to advance your response while the giver is still talking. Changes in opinion are more likely to occur when the giver feels understood and respected.

CLEAR Questions to Ask:

1. The purpose of the feedback:

1. 'How should I take this feedback—as an evaluation, coaching, advice, or an order?'
2. 'Is the feedback final or negotiable?'

2. The facts and impact of the feedback:

1. 'Can you tell me what you mean by the words…?'
2. 'Could you give me an example of the behaviour that concerns you?'
3. 'Can you help me understand how you came to that conclusion?'
4. 'Can you help me understand why this important?'
5. 'Who did you talk to arrive at your conclusion?'

3. Brainstorming actions:

1. 'Can you clarify what you would like me to do differently?'
2. 'What is the one thing I could do differently that would most help you?'

4. Be careful not to use sarcasm, loaded, or leading questions. Here are some examples of what not to say:

1. 'I seem to be doing everything wrong. Any more friendly advice you want to throw into the mix!?'
2. 'Isn't it true that I usually arrive on time?'

3. 'Do you think your feedback could be politically motivated?'
4. 'Do you actually think this is a fair conclusion?'

4.2 Repeat Back Words for Understanding

Showing empathy in a tense or uncomfortable discussion shows maturity and allows you to shift toward a more collaborative dialogue. If the giver feels listened to and in tune with the receiver, the outcome is more likely to be positive.

Tips for Listening:

1. Make notes.
2. Summarise what you have just heard the giver say to check for understanding and to demonstrate that you are genuinely listening.
3. Repeat back answers; this is especially key across cultures, where not everyone is equally skilled at speaking the language.

4.3 Take Responsibility for Actions

Be accountable and accept that nobody is perfect. We all make mistakes and there is a good possibility that you have—at the least—contributed to the problem in some way. Try to stay objective and as flexible as possible with your interpretation of the situation. Remember humans are too complex, and life is too messy, to get trapped in all or nothing thinking. To change and grow, we must accept that we are a bit of everything: trusting and suspicious, selfish and caring, speaking the truth and telling white lies, generous and jealous.

It's key to conclude the conversation with a clear commitment to do something specific to improve the situation. If we are not explicit, we often end up disappointed by a lack of progress.

Ideas for Action:

1. If you made a mistake say you are sorry—several times and in several ways—if needed.
2. Generate options that matter to both parties.
3. Focus on low-hanging fruit. Sometimes easy and obvious steps can have significant consequences. By trying to do everything at the same time, you can end up accomplishing nothing at all.
4. Experiment and try out the new behaviour. Sometimes it is easier to act our way into new ways of thinking than it is to think our way into new actions.

The Takeaways

1. Consider: Put Yourself in the Shoes of the Giver

1. Show empathy.
2. Unpack feedback for deeper meaning.
3. Separate the message from the messenger.

2. Awareness: Know Yourself

1. Recognise your emotions.
2. Be aware how you tend to deal with feedback.
3. Understand how others perceive you.

3. Listen: Control Yourself

1. Show confidence.
2. Control the impulse to act.
3. Stay open to new information.

4. Manage: Actively Question

1. Use the CLEAR steps for clarification.
2. Repeat back words for understanding.
3. Take responsibility for actions.

5

FEEDBACK UNDER TIME PRESSURE

If you think safety is expensive, try an accident.

Trevor Kletz

Keep Flying the Plane

When Captain Chesley Sullenberger and his crew had to manage a double engine failure after take-off, their work methods switched from 'normal' to 'emergency'. Although this sounds obvious, the chaos provoked by turbine breakdown (alarms going off, instruments failing, information overload, etc.), can make priority setting challenging. There is a real danger that stressed crews fixate on specific problems while forgetting more obvious issues like keeping the plane in the air. Therefore, the first thing that Captain Sullenberger did was take the flight controls from the First Officer, who had lost all his instruments. Only when the heavily damaged aircraft was on a safe flightpath did the crew shift attention to the damaged engines.

In cockpits of airliners, there is a clear distinction between normal and emergency situations, where different procedures apply. There is a shift from people-oriented leadership to task-oriented leadership.

The captain will maintain overall control of the situation with the input of every crew member. Communication speeds up and becomes direct and instructive. Feedback is instant and focused on trouble shooting and correcting mistakes. There is no time for egos; damage to relationships is repaired later.

Crew members are trained extensively for emergencies so they remain calm, confident and focused on the task at hand:

1. Declare the emergency.
2. Keep flying the plane.
3. Assess the problems.
4. Take action.
5. Debrief, to learn from mistakes and strengthen relationships.

In organisational life, there are also emergency situations where you need to act fast to solve problems, even though it may not be a question of life and death. Last-minute presentations, new deadlines, technology issues, competitive forces and changing regulations can all put immense pressure on teams to deliver results. When time is an issue, it is essential to keep the communication channels open, but filter out the clutter. The feedback loop becomes shorter so you can identify problems and solutions faster. It is particularly important to postpone the 'who is to blame' discussion until the debriefing; always focus on the immediate tasks to resolve the emergency situation.

Let's look at the CLEAR+CALM model in emergency mode. The team leader will play a strong coordinating role.

Tips for Giving Feedback under Pressure:

Constructive: Make sure everyone on the team is aware of the situation by declaring an emergency: 'People, we have an emergency. The servers are down and our customers can't get into our application'.

Language: Use clear language and ask people to confirm and repeat back the message. 'The team leaders have a meeting in 10 minutes to see how we get the application up and running. Does everyone understand? Any questions?'

Ask everyone to speak up and give their opinion using words that are difficult to ignore or brush aside: 'I'm concerned...', 'I'm uncomfortable...', 'We need to stop...'

Evaluate: Ask for input from the team and move to action. 'Any ideas or comments relevant to solving the problem?'

Action: Actions should be directed towards resolving the situation. 'So, do we all agree we should restart the server?'

Relation: Organise a debrief to understand what went wrong, learn from mistakes and restore relationships. ('So, how can we make sure that we properly test new code? We are the experts. If we can't stabilise the platform nobody can!').

Tips for Receiving Feedback under Pressure:

Consider: Be mindful that the giver may be in a stressful position. This is not the time to go into lengthy discussions about blame or create conflict. ('Ok, I understand the app is not working. What can I do?').

Awareness: Put emotions and defensiveness on hold. Focus on solving the problem and deal with relationships later. ('Ok, this would not be my approach, but I'm ready to work on a solution.').

Listen: Listening is hard in high-stress situations. We all have a tendency towards action ('Let's just do something!') before we fully understand the situation. Focus on troubleshooting and problem-solving. Relationship issues can wait until the situation is under control.

Manage: The team needs to be aware of all relevant information. The most junior team member could be the one with the most valuable information. Ask questions to clarify the situation and repeat back what you hear. 'Just to make sure I understand; we need to restart the server at 10.00 Singapore time. Is that correct?.' If you are worried about the situation, challenge the giver with words that are difficult to ignore or brush aside: 'I'm concerned that if we reset the server we could lose a lot of customer data'; 'I'm uncomfortable with resetting the server before we have talked with the developers.'

The Takeaways

- In emergency situations it important not to jump to conclusions or—worse—jump into action without understanding what is going on around you.
- Feedback is an essential channel for good situational awareness.
- The CLEAR+CALM model can also be used to navigate feedback under pressure. The steps are shorter to solve the problem as quickly, and safely, as possible.
- Once the situation is under control a debriefing allows the team to re-establish relationships and learn from emergencies, so they are better dealt with in the future.

6

POSITIVE FEEDBACK WORKS

Without a conscious effort to maintain recognition, the negative events will continually jump in line before the positive ones.

Rodd Wagner & James K. Harter

THE PRIMARY FOCUS of this book is giving and receiving feedback as a way to address problems and opportunities, but there's another type of feedback to improve performance: recognition and praise. We all like to be noticed and feel appreciated.

You would expect this type of feedback to be more frequent as it seems easier to do; who does not like to give good news? Unfortunately, this is not always the case.

Why?

1. **No news is good news.** We pay more attention to negative information: what is going wrong vs. what is going right.
2. **It is all about me.** We are all slightly selfish and more focused on receiving than giving. Highly competitive people in particular sometimes feel it takes away a bit of their own power to praise others.
3. **It is never good enough**. Sometimes we are afraid that people might slack off and become complacent if we tell them they are doing a great job.
4. **Not my strength.** We do not know how to do it and therefore avoid it.

Why We Love Feedback

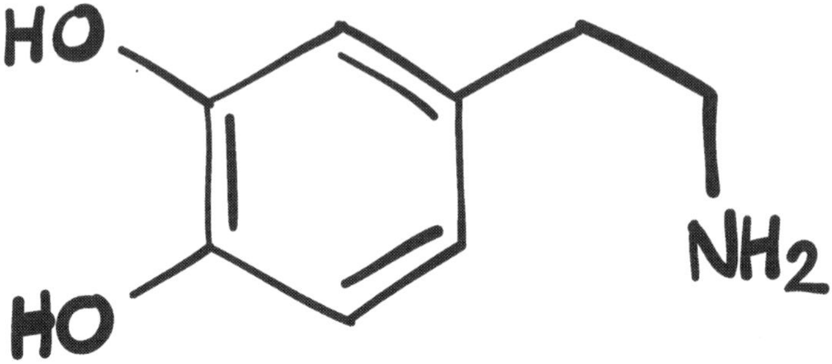

Any 'achievement' experience—winning a game, finishing a task, completing a project, reaching a goal—produces a hit of a neurotransmitter called dopamine which makes us feel joy and satisfaction. Our brain craves dopamine, driving the action that gets us the reward, thereby reinforcing and repeating behaviour, over and over again. This is why rewards are considered more effective than punishment and fear when it comes to modifying behaviour.

Positive words about our achievements also activate the regions of the brain related to rewards—so we are all positive feedback junkies. We deeply desire recognition and appreciation from the people around us: in our relationships, at work, offline or online. The more we get, the better we feel and the more we will do to get it again.

Technology has given us many more ways to seek out recognition and receive credit. It multiplies our channels for being liked far beyond close friends, colleagues or neighbours. So, we post a picture or a blog and wait for feedback; the better the comments, the more we post—feeding our dopamine addiction. There's nothing wrong with that—it's just an indication of how technology connects us and how robust and varied our social circles have become.

According to the Gallup organisation, employees who regularly receive positive feedback have fewer sick days, more satisfied customers, more productivity and generate higher revenue.[30] That's why Gallup asks: In the last seven days have you received recognition and praise for doing good work? in their engagement survey that thousands of companies use around the world. Positive feedback makes perfect business sense!

Positive Feedback Saves Fuel

Measuring fuel efficiency and giving positive feedback dramatically reduced kerosene consumption by Virgin Atlantic Pilots. A behavioural research study by three economists from the University of Chicago and the London School of Economics found that informing the pilots about fuel saving behaviours and giving them positive feedback on their performance resulted in savings of 21,500 tonnes of carbon and £3.3 million in fuel costs.[31] The study also found that pilots felt more satisfied with their jobs and 81% said they wanted more fuel-efficiency information in future. Captains and their crews have direct control over fuel load, efficient flight and efficient taxi.

Positive Feedback that Works

To improve performance using positive feedback, we need to first distinguish the two types of positive feedback.

- **Recognition—or a simple thank you for work well performed.** That doesn't mean the work needs to be exceptional. It is just a polite way of recognising that somebody has put time and energy into a task and they didn't go unnoticed. A simple 'thank-you' can be energising and motivating.
- **Praise for work exceptionally well performed.** Sometimes people go above and beyond normal levels of performance. They put in more time and effort to exceed goals. By praising such efforts, you recognise work and label it as outstanding, making people feel proud and admired.

Both types of feedback are important and will produce the dopamine fix we all crave, but it is important not to mix them up. If you say everything is amazing, it takes away the power to truly showcase exceptional performance. Note the difference between:

'Thank you for making the presentation!' and 'Thank you for making a presentation I will never forget!'

Tips for Giving Positive Feedback:

Use the CLEAR guidelines: Prepare, find the right timing and words, use facts and be direct:

- Clearly explain what the positive feedback is for. 'Thank you for the support you gave me in the meeting. I appreciate it!'
- Tailor the feedback to the person. Some people like to be praised in public, others in private. Some people like to be singled out; others prefer to be recognised as part of a team. Being aware of personal tastes and local cultures can mean the difference between motivating and embarrassing.
- Make sure feedback follows quickly after the event. By saving it for an annual performance review it loses a lot of its motivating power.
- Do not praise the person, but the behaviour. Although people may feel great when they hear they are a living example of excellence, it can destroy self-esteem if they fail later. Failing to live up to high personal expectations is a recipe for shame, guilt and stress.
- Make it sound like you mean it. We humans can sense if somebody is just going through the motions.

One Tip for Receiving Positive Feedback:

Stay CALM and accept any recognition or praise with a 'Thank you!'.

It's fine to show you are modest or a perfectionistic team player, but denying or downplaying your achievements is counterproductive. In some cultures, the pressure to remain out of the spotlight is stronger than in others. However, if you receive positive feedback, it is best to accept it and celebrate the moment. Gratitude shows respect, builds trust and reinforces the relationship. This way, both giver and receiver will get their dopamine dose and feel a sense of achievement.

The Takeaways

- Positive feedback is made up of recognition (a simple thank you) and praising exceptional achievements. Not everything can be exceptional.
- As humans, we need to feel noticed, appreciated and recognised.
- Positive feedback is proven to improve performance and engagement in the workplace.
- Despite the obvious benefit, it is not given regularly in organisations.
- Positive feedback is specific, timely, personal and genuine.
- It is important for giver and receiver to accept and celebrate positive feedback.

7

ASKING FOR FEEDBACK

I think it's very important to have a feedback loop, where you're constantly thinking about what you've done and how you could be doing it better.

Elon Musk

FEEDBACK IS NOT just something that must be suffered or managed; actively asking for feedback can have a profound impact on your performance.

Older generations were willing, or even happy, to wait for feedback until the annual performance review. The social media-savvy Millennials come into your office and ask for feedback and expect an answer.

Why Ask for Feedback?

1. **It improves performance.** We ask for feedback because it helps us do our job and reach our goals. In a dynamic world where a change of position, company and even career is the new normal, feedback brings us up to speed rapidly.
2. **It builds an accurate self-image.** With the help of others, I can adjust my self-view to realistic proportions, even if it feels uncomfortable or—temporarily—unpleasant.
3. **It shows courage, humility and trust in others.** I am human. Therefore, I make mistakes. Your feedback will help me grow.

Tips for Seeking Feedback Using CLEAR Steps:

1. **Constructive.** Reflect on what you want to ask and why you want to ask it. Prepare some questions to guide the feedback. Look for the right timing and

ask if it is convenient. Continuously interrupting busy people will stop their feedback fast.

2. **Language.** Use precise language to describe the context and the behaviour you want feedback on. Explain how the person's open and honest feedback can help you improve and that you are ready to listen to whatever they want to say.
3. **Evaluate.** Be prepared to hear bad news. When you expect endorsements and recognition, critical feedback can damage your cherished self-image and trigger defensiveness, at least for a moment. Control your response by remaining CALM: be empathic, be self-aware, listen and question for understanding.
4. **Action.** Follow up, follow up and follow up some more. Building up expectations by asking for feedback, but failing to follow up, is a great recipe for losing the trust and respect of the giver. If you do not intend to change anything it is better not to ask for feedback in the first place.
5. **Relationship.** If you get critical feedback, make sure the giver understands you do not feel hurt, disappointed or betrayed (even if you do). It takes courage to ask AND give open and honest feedback. Normalise the relationship by thanking the giver for his time and honesty. Then close the feedback discussion and move on to other issues, showing the giver that you are ok.

For this book, we asked several friendly readers to give us feedback on the first manuscript. After all, when you write about the benefits of feedback you must lead the way.

We followed our own rules as we took the time to explain the project and stressed we needed honest opinions to improve. We gave our feedback friends questions to think about and—again— assured them we were not going to feel disappointed or attacked if the feedback turned out to be negative: our relationship was safe.

When the feedback finally arrived, I was surprised at the intensity of my own defensive reactions. I felt irritated and embarrassed; maybe I was just not smart enough to write a book. I started to (over) explain myself and find excuses for mistakes I had made.

This is a normal reaction to feedback. If you find yourself feeling defensive, remember the CALM steps for taking in feedback. Here is what worked for me:

1. **Consider**. I put myself in the shoes of the giver. I had asked trusted friends to put time and effort into improving my work. They were there to help and probably felt a bit anxious about giving feedback to a friend who has been putting his heart and soul into his first book project.
2. **Awareness**. I know I have a tendency to defend my creative work. The more effort I put in, the more I push back. I also know that if I can sit with this painful feeling of feedback anxiety it goes away.
3. **Listen**. I force myself to stay calm by breathing, smiling and nodding; anything to show the giver I am interested and paying attention.
4. **Manage**. Once I feel calm I question the giver gently to fully understand and decide what to do with their comments.

By getting a taste of my own medicine, I realised how tough it is to deal with feedback even if you ask for it and seem prepared. The good news is that, with practice, it does get easier.

The result is a much better book and—after my initial dip in confidence—I firmly believe feedback is a gift, not a curse. Thank you!

One Tip, if You Are Asked for Feedback:

Recognise the courage it takes to ask for feedback. Then use the CLEAR steps to respond.

The Takeaways

- Asking for feedback is the best way to improve yourself and get better, especially in a rapidly changing world.
- Using the CLEAR part of the CLEAR+CALM model lets you effectively prepare and manage the asking process.
- Be prepared for the worst. Use the CALM steps to receive the feedback.
- Show gratitude and demonstrate progress to the giver. Visible results will lead to more and better feedback and it might stimulate others to try it themselves.
- Asking for feedback gets easier over time. Your confidence will grow.

8

CLEAR+CALM IN ACTION

Facts do not cease to exist because they are ignored.

Aldous Huxley

SCENARIO: GREY BEAUTY

WE WILL USE the Grey Beauty story to look at how people experience and interpret the same events in different ways. In the tips section we then analyse the feedback discussions, using the CLEAR+CALM steps.

As you will see, feedback can easily escalate and the dialogues do not always follow the steps in a particular order.

Sometimes the giver turns into the receiver, you might have to go back a step, or you can skip steps entirely.

Grey Beauty

Jasmin, a 25-year-old Spanish engineer and Project Manager of Grey Beauty, is about to present a new tulip that will last 100 times longer than any other, in the ground or in a vase. The technology behind Grey Beauty is highly innovative and could turn TULIPAN NORWAY AS into a market leader overnight. Jasmin has been coordinating with different departments to get Grey Beauty ready for market launch. So far everything has been kept top secret.

In the audience, team member Kari, R&D colleague Ricardo, Jasmine's boss Jeff, and the rest of the head office staff have turned up to listen to her. The Marketing Department have even invited some friendly customers and a journalist.

Jasmin has prepared the presentation on her own; it covers the entire project in great detail: background, opportunity, business case, etc.

She speaks fast as she goes through every single item. On slide 60, Jasmin shows the only image, a picture of Grey Beauty, following up with the last slide showing a launch schedule. She finishes 15 minutes over time.

Halfway during the presentation, some people start using their mobile phones and, towards the end, you can hear the muffled sound of people whispering to each other. The applause lasts about 2 seconds.

Jasmin walks off stage looking worried and stressed.

Profiles

JASMIN Background

Name: Jasmin Williams

Age: 34

Nationality: Spanish

Personality: Open, organised, but slightly insecure

Project Grey Beauty is Jasmin's first big job leading a team and she feels the pressure from all sides. On top of that her home life with a working husband and two small daughters keeps her busy; she feels and looks exhausted. Determined not to forget anything she decides to include every single detail of the project on the slides and memorise her notes. She had tried to show Jeff her draft but he seemed busy and she did not want to bother him. She also did not want anyone to think she could not handle the pressure!

JEFF Background

Name: Jeff Rodes

Age: 50

Nationality: American

Personality: Routine, organised, introvert and usually worried about something

Jeff has been looking forward to this presentation. With the right support for Grey Beauty he will get a bigger budget and more responsibility for his department. He has been feeling stuck in his job for the last year; this could be his big break into something new and exciting. Eager to empower Jasmin and show his trust he did not ask to see the presentation before launch. In his last performance review his boss had asked him to delegate more to his team and give them space to grow.

KARI Background

Name: Kari Snillegaard

Age: 24

Nationality: Norwegian

Personality: Adventurer, flexible, extrovert and secure

Kari loves the fact that flowers make life more colourful. She has been working overtime to get Grey Beauty ready for launch. The nights, the weekends; it has all been worth it. She likes her team but finds it difficult to get closer to Jasmin, who never seems to stay around for long. Kari offered her help with the presentation and secretly hoped she could present some slides, but Jasmin declined without any explanation. Kari knew she was doing a good job, but she still felt that a simple 'thank you' from her boss was not too much to ask for.

RICARDO Background

Name: Ricardo Batista

Age: 54

Nationality: Peruvian/Japanese

Personality: Calm, secure and friendly, outgoing

Ricardo has been with the company since the start, 20 years ago in Oslo. For the last five years he has led the R&D department and is on his way to retiring in a couple of years. Ricardo is respected and the go-to person for advice or help.

Ricardo likes his fatherly coaching role in the company, but still struggles with giving more critical feedback. In order to avoid hurting people he usually tells white lies. He has noticed that the younger staff initially were not afraid to ask how they were doing, but seldom came back for more feedback.

Discussions and Analysis

In the coffee break after the presentation Jasmin has the following discussions:

Discussion 1

With American supervisor Jeff, surrounded by the management team.

JEFF: That was a disaster. The entire audience was bored.

JASMIN: Well, maybe you could have helped me prepare?!

JEFF: Oh, so now it's my fault?

JASMIN: No, don't worry; nothing is ever your fault.

Feedback Analysis 1

JEFF: That was a disaster. The entire audience was bored.

CLEAR Tips for Jeff:

1. **Constructive**

   - Jeff should not give feedback when he is feeling angry or emotional. Take time to calm down and be prepared. As a leader he is also a role model for productive feedback.

- Remember the purpose of feedback: helping people perform better. This was criticism, not feedback.
- Jeff should be careful with feedback in public. Better to choose a quiet place and have enough time for a proper discussion.
- Put yourself in Jasmin's shoes. Jeff knows she has been working hard at work and at home. She is very sensitive and a little insecure, so her first big presentation will create stress.
- Jasmin is Spanish and tends to look up to supervisors for direction and approval, even if Jeff has told her several times that she is running her own shop and he trusts her.

2. **Language**

- Jeff should choose his words carefully to avoid feedback coming across as a personal attack. Your comments might make Jasmin feel she has a problem with her character, not with her presentation.
- Be careful with highly subjective generalisations (the entire audience) and dramatic statements (disaster). Jasmin is already hard enough on herself; there's no need to humiliate her.

JASMIN: Well, maybe you could have helped me prepare.

CALM Tips for Jasmin:

1. **Consider**

    - Jasmin should put herself in the shoes of Jeff. Jeff might feel embarrassed in front of a big audience. He might also blame himself for not checking the presentation. Maybe Jeff tends to overreact when he feels insecure.

2. **Awareness**

    - Jasmin should also reflect on her own reaction and emotions. Why does she let Jeff get to her so easily? Is *she* actually the one who feels she is a disaster?

3. **Listen**

    - By remaining calm and curious you would have a great opportunity to show she can control her emotions under pressure, even in difficult and unfair circumstances.

4. **Manage**

    - By asking Jeff for a clarification she could have explored for better feedback and helped him calm down.

- If Jeff feels very upset and emotional he is not likely to think straight. Better choose a different time and place to continue the conversation.

JEFF: Oh, so now it is my fault?

CALM Tips for Jeff:

1. Listen

- Jeff needs to find a way to take control of his emotions. His monkey is jumping all over the place. If he can somehow recognise this, he could put it back in the box.
- If Jeff cannot regain his composure it is better to break off the discussion and continue at a later date.

JASMIN: No, don't worry; nothing is ever your fault.

GAME OVER

Discussion 2

With Norwegian team member and subordinate Kari, in a quiet corner.

KARI: Thank you for mentioning us in your speech.

JASMIN: What do you mean?

KARI: Typical, never mind.

JASMIN: So you think I only care about me?!

Feedback Analysis 2

KARI: Thank you for mentioning us in your speech.

CLEAR Tips for Kari:

1. **Constructive**

    - Kari picks a good place for feedback away from the crowd. However, she can see her boss is distracted and worried by her performance so this might not be the time to talk to her.

    - Keep in mind that Jasmin has told the team she

struggles with positive feedback, but she is really proud of their achievements.

2. **Language**

- Kari uses sarcasm to tell Jasmin she would have liked to be recognised. By being more direct and open with her feedback it would be easier for Jasmin to remain calm and learn.

JASMIN: What do you mean?

CLEAR Tips for Jasmin:

1. **Consider**

- Jasmin should keep in mind that Kari has worked hard on this project, so far without much recognition. Kari likes to be involved in everything and Jasmin has not had much time to spend with her.

2. **Awareness**

- Jasmin knows she is not very good at recognising people. She has hired the best to do their best. On top of that Jasmin does not care much for recognition herself.

3. **Listen**

   - Jasmin should be able to pick up the underlying message through the sarcasm: Kari would have liked to be recognised for her role in the project.

4. **Manage**

   - By questioning Kari she could find out more. However, her very short question sounds defensive and irritated. This could upset Kari further.

KARI: Typical, never mind.

CLEAR Tips for Kari:

1. **Evaluate**

   - Kari should try to remain calm and reflect on Jasmin's answer. Her boss is visibly stressed out and tired after the presentation. This might not be the right time to talk about this.

   - Although Jasmin's question sounds irritated Kari has no reason to believe that Jasmin wants all the attention and glory for herself: always give people the benefit of the doubt when it comes to intentions.

2. Language

- The word 'typical' can easily be interpreted as a personal attack on Jasmin (character assassination). 'Never mind' also sounds sarcastic and shows disappointment, which can provoke shame and defensiveness in Jasmin.

JASMIN: So you think I only care about me?!

GAME OVER

Discussion 3

With Ricardo, her peer and head of R&D, the day after her presentation.

JASMIN: Tell me Ricardo, how did I do?

RICARDO: Well... Ok I guess.

JASMIN: Come on, we all need feedback to improve. I really trust your opinion.

RICARDO: Ok, your work on Grey Beauty has been outstanding. Now your presentation needs to be the same. I think we could shorten it and put in some images to keep the audience on their toes. We could practice it with my team next Friday. What do you think?

JASMIN: Thank you, that's great feedback! Let's sit down and review the slides tonight. I'll order your favourite pizza!

Feedback Analysis 3

JASMIN: Tell me Ricardo, how did I do?

CLEAR Tips for Jasmin:

1. **Constructive**

    - Jasmin decides to ask for feedback when she has had time to calm down.

- As she knows Ricardo is always afraid of hurting people she could have stressed how important his (honest) opinion is for her to get better. To avoid putting Ricardo on the spot she could have sent him a quick email before walking in.

2. Language

- Her question is open and sounds genuine. No problematic or vague words. She is not fishing for compliments.

RICARDO: Well ...ok, I guess.

CLEAR Tips for Ricardo:

1. Constructive

- Ricardo probably feels a bit caught by surprise. He has not been able to prepare for this uncomfortable question. After all, it was not Jasmin's best performance.

2. Language

- Ricardo uses vague language, probably to soften the blow. It is better to recognise Jasmin as a key player and still be direct with Jasmin about her presentation.

JASMIN: Come on, we all need feedback to improve. I really trust your opinion.

CLEAR Tips for Jasmin:

1. **Constructive**

   - Jasmin knows Ricardo is uncomfortable and makes sure she builds a safe environment for Ricardo to speak up. His image and their relationship will not be damaged.

RICARDO: Ok, your work on Grey Beauty has been outstanding. Now your presentation needs to be the same. I think we could shorten it and put in some images to keep the audience on their toes. We could practice it with my team next Friday. What do you think?

CLEAR Tips for Ricardo:

1. **Language**

   - Ricardo put Jasmin at ease by recognising her work on the project. He also avoided the 'but' word which could have diminished his earlier compliment.

   - By using 'I' Ricardo takes responsibility for his statement and he remains objective.

2. **Action**

- Ricardo does not dwell on mistakes. He knows that Jasmin has already spent a lot of time thinking about her presentation. Instead, he offers a desirable future where the presentation is outstanding and keeps the audience on their toes.
- He offers some suggestions but involves Jasmin by asking her for her ideas.
- He offers to set a deadline, looking for a clear commitment from Jasmin.

JASMIN: Thank you, that is great feedback! Let's sit down and review the slides. Are you free tonight? I'll order your favourite pizza!

CALM Tips for Jasmin:

1. **Consider**

- Always thank people for their feedback, even if the message sounds offensive or hurtful. It shows courage and a genuine interest in improving yourself. This time Ricardo has done a very good job so Jasmin stays in learning mode!

2. Manage

- Jasmin takes responsibility and shows her commitment to improve by suggesting immediate action, but waiting for Ricardo to agree.

WELL MANAGED!

PART III: LEADING FEEDBACK

9

CREATING A PSYCHOLOGICALLY SAFE WORK ENVIRONMENT

Designated leaders need to cultivate leadership skills in each team member by giving others the confidence, the tools, the freedom and the accountability that empowers each person to take on more responsibility and to make critical decisions when the path ahead may not be clear-cut—especially if the designated leader is no longer able to do the job.

Alison Levine

THE TERM 'PSYCHOLOGICAL safety' denotes the idea that members of a team trust each other and feel secure to give feedback, without fear of committing professional suicide. When team members feel respected, they will worry less about being rejected and more about speaking up with ideas, questions, concerns, or mistakes.

Google Discovers the Value of Psychological Safety

In 2012, Google started Project Aristotle to find the recipe for top team performance. They gathered some of the company's best researchers, statisticians, organisational psychologists, sociologists and engineers to review academic studies about teamwork.

The project team discovered some work by a group of psychologists from Carnegie Mellon and the Massachusetts Institute of Technology in 2008 on 'collective intelligence'. This research concluded that the members of the top teams treat each other well. How?

1. Everyone gets a chance to talk and speaks roughly the same amount.

2. Team members score high on emotional intelligence, especially empathy, or the capacity to tune into what other people are feeling.

These two behaviours provide a sense of psychological safety, a term Harvard Professor Amy C. Edmondson talks about in her ground-breaking book, *Teaming: How Organisations Learn, Innovate, and Compete in the Knowledge Economy*. It describes a team climate of trust and respect in which people feel safe to speak up and have difficult conversations.

A survey of Google's internal personnel data proved that psychological safety, more than anything else, was critical to making a team work in Google.

Project Aristotle showed Google that to be fully engaged at work, you need to feel safe to speak up and share things without fear. Efficiency is not everything. Using hard data to validate the importance of soft skills makes it easier to train and get buy-in from engineers and scientists who are not always comfortable talking about feelings.[32]

We Are All in Charge

The CLEAR+CALM model provides the skills and behaviour to give and receive feedback in a respectful way. To make sure that this feedback keeps flowing, it is the formal responsibility of the team leader to create and promote a feedback-safe environment. However, in today's dynamic world, leadership itself has become a team sport, continuously re-distributed to the most qualified person for each situation and task. It is, therefore, a team's collective responsibility to establish and maintain a climate of open, honest and respectful communication. When it comes to feedback, we are all leaders.

Here's how it works, using the acronym **SAFE**:

- **S**etting boundaries.
- **A**ctivating feedback.
- **F**ailing better.
- **E**mpowering the team.

Step 1: Setting Boundaries

When leaders and teams are clear about what is acceptable behaviour in the workplace, everyone feels more psychologically safe than when boundaries are vague or unpredictable. Clearly state that speaking up and listening respectfully are expected team norms. Hold yourself and your colleagues accountable for bad behaviour—such as remaining silent, criticising, not listening, humiliating, ridiculing, etc.—by naming and correcting these behaviours.

Step 2: Activating Feedback

Leaders should actively model, invite and reward their teams for speaking up. By openly endorsing and using the CLEAR+CALM model, they teach every team member how to give and receive feedback in an effective and respectful manner.

It's especially important that teams feel that leaders are committed to following-up on ideas and concerns to avoid a 'why bother' reaction. Research has found that managers' failure to follow up increased their subordinates' belief that speaking up is futile by 30%. If managers closed the loop, their teams spoke up more frequently.[33]

Step 3: Failing Better

There is nothing more disarming than when leaders allow team members to see their 'not so perfect' side. It reminds us that we are all human and we all make mistakes; it makes us feel closer and safer. Unfortunately, many leaders think that showing vulnerability makes them look unprofessional and weak.

Tips for showing fallibility and vulnerability:

- Show a tolerance of mistakes by acknowledging your own fallibility. Highlight failures as learning opportunities instead of grounds for punishment or criticism.

- Openly display gaps in knowledge as opportunities to learn. When leaders admit that they don't know something, their genuine display of humility encourages other team members to follow their example without having to worry about being seen as ignorant, incompetent, negative or disruptive.

- Include yourself in the feedback. By using inclusive language ('I tend to struggle with recognising people, too.'), the receiver will be less likely to treat the feedback as a personal attack. It also shows that you do not feel superior or better.

Step 4: Empowering the Team

By nature, hierarchies limit low-ranking group members from voicing their opinions and concerns. In contrast, when lower-ranked colleagues feel empowered to speak up and share relevant information, everyone becomes responsible for identifying critical errors and preventing problems.

Effective leaders push their teams to share crucial information and to speak up—to exercise control and independence and to work without overbearing supervision. By promoting equality and playing down their power, team members are more motivated to disagree openly with their leaders and colleagues and less likely to be intimidated by hierarchy and rigid organisational structures.

Challenging Authority

On 27 March 1977, technical and non-technical factors led up to one of the worst accidents in civil aviation to date. The captain of a KLM aircraft decided to take-off while a Pan Am aircraft was still on the same runway in Tenerife, Spain. Crash investigators discovered that the authoritarian behaviour of the captain, in combination with other factors, played a significant role in the cause of the accident. The crew was hesitant to challenge their highly respected captain even though it could—and did—kill them.

This accident sparked a transformational training effort, which is now deeply embedded in all training programs at KLM and other airlines. Never ever should a crew member, regardless of rank and or seniority, be allowed to play such an overpowering role in the operation of an aircraft. This awareness has been one of the foundations of the impressive safety record of KLM and many other airlines during the past decades.

Tips to Empowering:

- Reduce the emphasis of hierarchy levels—or eliminate them altogether—as a means of minimising the 'us vs. them' mentality. Doing so will increase the sense of team spirit and productivity.
- Limit or decrease signs and symbols of hierarchy, such as offices, suit and ties, company cars.
- Ask for feedback and encourage all team members to speak up and share ideas regularly.
- Call on each person in meetings to contribute ideas one by one.
- Recognise people publicly for speaking up.
- Follow up on concerns and ideas.
- Do not allow questions or interruptions until each contributor has finished speaking.
- Call for written ideas or contributions before meetings and discuss them anonymously, acknowledging the author when his or her idea is adopted.

Who Should Use SAFE?

As with the CALM and CLEAR model, work SAFE applies to three overlapping groups of users:

- Individuals—leaders and followers—who want to improve their influencing skills to promote feedback, even without the title to back it up.
- Teams who want to stimulate feedback to improve their performance. In this case, SAFE is adopted as a group norm.
- Organisations that want to build feedback right into the corporate culture.

The Takeaways

- It is the role of leaders AND their teams to actively create and promote a feedback-SAFE environment.
- SAFE stands for:
  1. **Setting Boundaries**: Make it clear that everyone is expected to give and receive feedback.
  2. **Activating Feedback**: Use and role model the CLEAR+CALM steps.
  3. **Failing Better**: Openly admit to mistakes and acknowledge knowledge gaps as learning opportunities.

4. **Empowering the Team**. Encourage the team to speak up and take decisions in their area of expertise.

- Organisations who want a 'feedback safe' culture need to support and train everyone in the organisation, starting, but not stopping, with top management.

PART IV: THE FUTURE OF FEEDBACK IN ORGANISATIONS

10

FORMAL FEEDBACK

People want to know on an ongoing basis ... Am I moving in the right direction? Do you think I'm progressing? Nobody's going to wait for an annual cycle to get that feedback.

Pierre Nanterme

Pierre Nanterme, the CEO of Accenture, is right. His company is a good example of an international knowledge company that depends on smart people thinking and working together. If their consultants do not talk to each other about problems and opportunities—across hierarchies and cultures—their intellectual horsepower will not be fast enough to help customers succeed in a complex future.

However, Pierre is wrong when he says 'Nobody's going to wait for an annual cycle to get feedback'. Millions of workers around the world are waiting for feedback every day and when it finally arrives it is usually in the form of an annual performance review.

Let's look at two examples of feedback systems that organisations use: the performance review and the engagement survey.

Why do we use them?

1. Promoting individual performance, learning and development.
2. Mapping and storing employee information.
3. Developing stimulating work environments where people feel safe and motivated.

The Performance Review

Performance reviews have been used by employers to make employees more accountable and productive. They are designed to work from the top down to 'push and pull' the best, the worst and anyone in between to achieve more. Once or twice a year we sit down and have a 'well prepared open discussion' about what goes to plan and what needs to be improved. However, they now often cause as many problems as they solve. Research suggests that more than one in three formal feedback sessions results in a decrease in job performance rather than the expected increase.[34]

Why Are Performance Reviews Outdated?

- They're periodic and no longer reflect the dynamic circumstances most organisations operate in. If you save up issues for discussion at the annual performance appraisal and don't deal with them as they arise, it is already too late.

- Many companies merely train managers to comply with the process instead of developing managers to coach employees.

- To avoid defensive and angry employees, managers avoid the discussion or soften the message to make it sound more positive than it is. Many managers are unconfident in their roles as evaluators of employee performance and so they struggle with giving quality feedback.

- Linking performance to some form of ranking can be particularly damaging inside knowledge

> companies that thrive on expertise, collaboration and transparency. Knowledge workers need incentives to collaborate and be creative, yet forced rankings and secret talent ratings produce the opposite behaviour: competition and politics.

Over the last 22 years, I have participated in this awkward ritual as a worker and a manager. At best these sessions officially summarised what we—giver and receiver—already knew because we had talked about the good and the bad many times before. At worst a performance review turned into a painful and lengthy negotiation, squeezing one year of facts and fiction into one crucial hour that could severely impact your professional future. Exhausted—both as a giver and receiver—I would need weeks to rebuild the relationship, or what was left of it.

Improving the Performance Review

Formal feedback requires careful preparation to focus on the facts and maintain relationships. It requires a complex balance of honesty, humility and humanity: the 'carefrontational' approach'. Excellent interpersonal skills and job expertise are essential, for givers and receivers alike.

The better the relationship between the giver and the receiver, the easier it is to deliver and respond to feedback. Trust and good intentions are the ingredients for a productive conversation. However, there is a fine line between love and hate. Make sure you follow the CLEAR+CALM steps to avoid feelings of hurt, betrayal and anger.

Tips for Giving Feedback in Formal Performance Reviews:

Study and use the CLEAR+CALM model for giving and receiving feedback. Some specific steps to keep in mind:

Constructive

1. The purpose and the goal of feedback should be clearly understood by both parties.
2. Feedback delivered for developmental purposes is best separated from the more administrative or reward-oriented feedback. Nobody is going to be very attentive to feedback after hearing they will not be getting a bonus.
3. The feedback should be private and confidential, to protect both the giver and the receiver.
4. Don't overwhelm the receiver with bad news; focus on a limited number of developmental needs per session.
5. Include both positive and developmental feedback in the review.

Language

1. Begin with a self-appraisal to increase your involvement and get buy-in.
2. The words—and the message in general—should be factual, respectful, constructive and leading towards improvement.

3. Focus on observed behaviours rather than the receiver's character.

Evaluate

1. Be patient; do not try to force opinion or agreement. We all need time to absorb, reflect and accept information.

Action

1. Emphasise a focus on learning—that it is all about a better future and not an unproductive past.
2. Build confidence in the ability to change behaviour.
3. Seek consensus on the way forward, or schedule a new meeting if emotions run too high.
4. Goals should be challenging, specific and realistic.
5. When you are dealing with the low performance of a high potential, the focus should be on improving skills.
6. With lower ability levels, improving performance should involve clear and realistic goals and restructuring the job around strengths instead of weaknesses.

Measuring Job Engagement

Apart from the—top-down—performance reviews of individual employees, companies are also using bottom-up feedback systems to measure and stimulate the motivation of the workforce.

Traditional satisfaction surveys ask for feedback on everything from the quality of the cafeteria to salary to the relationship we have with bosses and team members.

The main problem with these types of surveys is that they take time to complete and are hard to follow up. Initially the results receive a lot of attention; top management promises to address the issues and Human Resources is made responsible for finding solutions. One year later nothing has changed because HR seldom has the capacity or influence to follow through on the actions that are necessary.

At the beginning of this century, the term 'engagement' took over from 'satisfaction' to focus on a more limited set of questions that measure the level of emotional commitment people have to their job. As we discussed in the introduction to this book, Gallup has found that the better people feel about their work, the better they do their job. The responsibility for following up on the results lies with the team, instead of them having to rely on HR. I have seen teams improving the way they work, provided everyone feels safe to discuss the issues openly and honestly.

The only problem that remains is that engagement surveys are usually limited to one or two measuring points a year. Moreover, these systems are expensive and time-consuming to manage, especially for bigger companies.

The Future of Feedback

Over the past few years, more and more companies are moving away from their traditional feedback systems towards a culture of continuous feedback. Given that business is in a constant state of flux—with shifting goals and employees moving between different teams and projects—traditional feedback systems do not seem to make much sense anymore.

GE, Adobe, Accenture, Expedia and Microsoft and dozens of other knowledge organisations have abandoned the annual performance review to 'rehumanize' the relationship between employees and their bosses, especially after noticing an uptick of high-potential employees leaving right after the annual round of meetings. Europe's biggest performance review software-maker, SAP, ditched its annual review process as it prevents constructive dialogue. 'Grading workers did not work. People are open to feedback, also to harsh criticism, until the moment you start giving scores. Then the shutters go down', said HR head Wolfgang Fassnacht. SAP is currently testing a new process, which includes more regular check-in talks, and hopes to implement it for all of its 80,000 employees next year.

We have found that merely abandoning an outdated system without training people to give and receive regular feedback does not work. Moreover, the company still needs to track and record employee performance over time to keep an eye on talent and learning needs.

Technology Can Provide Direction

Technology has created a 'feedback economy'. We can rate almost anything: restaurants, airlines, automobiles, doctors, plumbers and the list goes on. Just as customer feedback has transformed and improved the customer experience, employee feedback is changing the employee experience. Imagine an app on your phone where you can immediately rate the work of a colleague or ask for comments about your own achievements. The company will have an aggregated view of the trends and can choose to publish rankings to recognise performance.

Online feedback sounds promising, but technology alone does not build a feedback culture. In fact, introducing technology without understanding the dynamics and the skills needed for feedback may even make the situation worse.

Why?

- If people don't feel safe or skilled offline posting feedback or ratings online is not going to happen. Just because there are tools or channels does not mean people will use them.

- Face-to-face communication is still the gold standard of feedback and healthy relationships. We can listen to what is said and we can observe the person who says it. Excessive use of social media tools leads to isolation and poor relationships.

- Tools and apps can easily be misused and manipulated. We can fall into the like for like trap, where gaming the system becomes a sport. Feedback now becomes a tradable commodity to boost reputation, regardless of whether the recognition is valid.

- Anonymity is a mixed blessing as it does not foster a culture where people feel safe and confident to be open and honest with each other. In fact, it may do the opposite.

- Allowing people to publish feedback anonymously or using a fake name strips away their responsibility for providing reasonable and respectful comments.

- Online feedback generates impressive real-time amounts of data. However, it can lead to spending too much time overthinking a situation so that we never take action. Analysis paralysis creates an illusion that something is being done because it looks factual and smart.

Using technology alone will not change behaviour. People might play along, but it will not last. Technology in combination with training and other forms of communication will deliver results. First, we need to become aware of the dynamics of feedback. Secondly, we need the skills for giving and receiving feedback in a productive and respectful way. Only when we are aware and skilled can we use technology to practice and provide feedback.

Tips for Using Technology to Promote Feedback:

1. Train people to give and receive feedback before introducing feedback technology.
2. Mix online feedback with more personal offline feedback.
3. Set ground rules for appropriate topics and language in online environments. It's important for everyone to realise that some comments may even provoke legal issues.
4. Complex and emotionally loaded issues are better discussed in person.
5. Do not to say anything online you would not tell a person face-to-face.
6. Describe the facts, using direct and clear words.

Remember that once you push the submit button the receiver—and possibly the rest of the organisation—are going to have it in writing.

7. Do not allow anyone to sign off feedback with a nickname. Treat people like adults and hold them responsible for their actions.
8. Use a common language, unless everyone is familiar with internet acronyms and chat jargon.
9. Make sure that feedback is followed up with action. The ability to quickly send and receive feedback does not mean anything changes.
10. Be careful with anonymity. It may be that people feel safer speaking up when their identity remains confidential, but this may reinforce the culture of secrecy we are trying to break down in the first place. In our experience, most employees don't believe that surveys are anonymous.
11. Make sure you are aware of the local legal regulations and labour agreements which govern the collection and use of employee data. Big Data analytics, or mining people data, is being hyped as one of the most significant trends in Human Resources, but misuse of data can have serious trust and legal implications.
12. Work with credible and neutral data scientists to

discover trends beyond the obvious usage statistics. Data can easily be misinterpreted.

The Takeaways

- Traditional feedback systems periodically capture and store feedback to improve performance, manage talent and build engaging workplaces.
- To deal with rapidly changing and complex environments organisations are creating feedback cultures based on continuous open and honest feedback.
- Social media technology for the workplace can promote the use of feedback, provided everyone is trained and there is a healthy dose of face-to-face communication.
- The CLEAR+CALM model provides the steps for formal and informal feedback, both offline and online.

11

CONCLUSION

I've learned one thing—people who know the least always seem to know it the loudest.

Andy Capp

IN A DYNAMIC world, feedback is crucial for any organisation that depends on knowledge work, learning and innovation.

If we cannot speak our minds or listen to others, we keep making the same mistakes over and over again. Silence in organisations may not kill, but slowly damages performance; think of it as death by a thousand things not said or said poorly. However, silence is only part of the problem. We also need to listen, reflect and act on the feedback we receive. Only when giver and receiver agree on action and follow-up do things improve.

Overcoming the Barriers to Feedback

In Chapter 1, we started off by exploring our mental software and how universal human drives, culture and personality, can trigger behaviour that limits feedback:

- **Staying Silent.** You or your team members may have developed a 'why bother' attitude or do not want to run the risk of being seen as ignorant, negative, harsh or hypocritical. People have a primeval instinct to respect authority, so challenging a person higher in rank can feel disrespectful and, in some organisations, outright dangerous.
- **Confusing Opinions with Facts.** When you do feel safe and confident enough to speak up, you may still confuse your opinions with the facts. Human biases and stereotypes distort reality, usually in our favour. Human beings are not as rational and clear as we like to think.
- **Choosing the Wrong Words.** Tone of voice, word choice and body language can unintentionally come off as impolite or hurtful. Vague language can be misunderstood and trigger confusion, especially in a multicultural environment.
- **Holding on to Inflated Self-views.** We tend to regard ourselves as a bit better and smarter than the rest of the world. It is therefore not so strange

that feedback can come across as unfair, untrue or disrespectful.

- **Defensiveness.** Although the rational brain is keen to absorb new knowledge, the emotional brain can easily interpret feedback as an attack. We fight back, we escape, or use more refined defence mechanisms to protect ourselves.

To overcome these behavioural barriers to feedback, we introduced a common sense approach that works across hierarchies and cultures: the CLEAR+CALM model.

The words CLEAR and CALM by themselves provide the essence of good feedback: give feedback clearly and receive feedback calmly. On a deeper level, every letter provides an essential step for giving and receiving feedback.

CLEAR Steps for Giving Feedback

1. **Constructive: Prepare the Case.**
    1. Be clear about the purpose of the feedback.
    2. Choose the right time and place for feedback.
    3. Take into account the position of the receiver.
2. **Language: Words Matter.**
    1. Use positive language.
    2. Use direct and action-focused statements.
    3. Use relevant facts.

3. **Evaluate: Manage Reactions.**
    1. Listen calmly.
    2. Give the benefit of the doubt.
    3. Understand your contribution to the problem.
4. **Action: Reach an Agreement.**
    1. Focus on a desired future.
    2. Involve the receiver.
    3. Brainstorm SMART goals.
5. **Relationship: Move on.**
    1. Re-establish the relationship.
    2. Offer a fresh start.
    3. Ask for feedback on feedback.

CALM Steps for Receiving Feedback

1. **Consider: Put Yourself in the Shoes of the Giver.**
    1. Show empathy.
    2. Unpack feedback for deeper meaning.
    3. Separate the message from the messenger.
2. **Awareness: Know Yourself.**
    1. Recognise your emotions.
    2. Be aware how you tend to deal with feedback.
    3. Understand how others perceive you.

3. **Listen: Control Yourself.**
    1. Show confidence.
    2. Control the impulse to act.
    3. Stay open to new information.
4. **Manage: Actively Question.**
    1. Use the CLEAR steps for clarification.
    2. Repeat back words for understanding.
    3. Take responsibility for actions.

The CLEAR+CALM model can be used for giving and receiving developmental feedback, positive feedback and in asking for feedback.

To support the CLEAR+CALM model we also introduced steps to create a feedback-safe environment where people feel confident to speak up and listen. When it comes to SAFE, leaders go first, but the entire team is responsible for making it happen.

SAFE Steps for Creating a Safe Environment

- **Setting boundaries**: Make it clear that everyone is expected to give and receive feedback.
- **Activating feedback**: Use and role model the CLEAR+CALM steps.

- **Failing Better:** Openly admit to mistakes and acknowledge knowledge gaps as learning opportunities.
- **Empowering the Team**: Encourage the team to speak up and take decisions in their area of expertise.

To deal with rapidly changing environments, organisations are starting to build feedback into their culture. New social media technologies are replacing traditional periodic Performance reviews and Engagement surveys. However, introducing digital tools without training in feedback first is useless. The CLEAR+CALM model provides the steps for productive formal and informal feedback, both offline and online.

We hope this book can serve as a starting point to improving the most important form of communication for learning, innovation and vibrant teamwork: feedback. Without the courage to speak and the capacity to listen, regardless of rank or culture, any type of change is doomed to fail fast. In contrast, build on a strong foundation of feedback and performance will follow; today, tomorrow and in the future.

BE
CLEAR
STAY
CALM

ACKNOWLEDGEMENTS

There are so many people who have contributed to the making of this book, both directly and indirectly, that we would need another chapter to list them. Therefore, we would rather say a big thank you to everyone who has helped, rather than leave someone out.

Special thanks go to our readers (the feedbackers) who allowed themselves to be sucked into reading and commenting on the many versions of this book and who have all given incredible feedback: Alan Rinzler, Anna Kofoed, Brigitte ten Dam, Carmen Ferrero Sanchez, Daniel del Olmo, Dick Stuyfzand, Dorus Evekink, Eric Hooftman, Hayder Al-Deen, João Mendes, Kyle Mulligan, Lisa Tener, Michiel van Straaten, Paul Evekink, Sophie Evekink and Stephane Pingaud.

We would also like to thank the great people in Amadeus for their inspiration and support. HCB-EBE teams: you rock!

Finally, we would like to thank you for reading our book. We hope that *Feedback First* will boost performance at work and home.

Never stop learning.

September, 2016

BIBLIOGRAPHY & FURTHER READING

Adkins, A. (2016, January 13). *Employee Engagement in U.S. Stagnant in 2015*. Retrieved June 6, 2016, from Gallup.com: http://www.gallup.com/poll/188144/employee-engagement-stagnant-2015.aspx

Adkins, A. (2016, May 11). *What Millennials Want From Work and Life*. Retrieved June 6, 2016, from Gallup: http://www.gallup.com/businessjournal/191435/millennials-work-life.aspx?g_source=EMPLOYEE_ENGAGEMENT&g_medium=topic&g_campaign=tiles

Anicich, E. M., Swaab, R. I., & Galinsky, A. D. (2015, February). Hierarchical cultural values predict success and mortality in high-stakes teams. *PNAS, 112*(5), 1338-1343.

Armstrong, A. (2012). The Art of Feedback. *The Learning System, 7*(4), pp. 3-5.

Ashford, S. J., Blatt, R., & Vande Walle, D. (2003). Reflections on the Looking Glass: A Review of Research on Feedback-Seeking Behavior in Organizations. *Journal of Management, 29*(6), 773-799.

Bendahana, S., Zehndera, C., Pralongc, F. P., & Antonakisa, J. (2015, April). Leader corruption on power and testosterone. *The Leadership Quarterly, 26*(2), 101-122.

Bersin, J. (2015, July 26). *Feedback is the Killer App: A*

New Market and Management Model Emerges. Retrieved from www.Forbes.com: http://www.forbes.com/sites/joshbersin/2015/08/26/employee-feedback-is-the-killer-app-a-new-market-emerges/print/

Blackburn, S., Ryerson, S., Weiss, L., Wilson, S., & Wood, C. (2011). *How do I implement complex change at scale?* McKinsey & Company, Organizational Practice. McKinsey & Company.

Burnett, D. (2016). *The Idiot Brain.* London: Guardian Books.

Bushe, G. R. (2010). *Clear Leadership.* Boston: Davies-Black.

Cannon, M., & Witherspoon, R. (2005). Actionable feedback: Unlocking the power of learning and performance improvement. *Academy of Management Executive, 19*(2).

Carter, R. (2009). *The Brain Book.* London: Dorley Kindersley Limited.

Childless, J. R. (2013). *Leverage.* London: Principia Associates.

CorpGov-SVC. (2016, July 21). *Comonsense Corporate Governance Principles.* Retrieved from http://www.governanceprinciples.org/: http://www.governanceprinciples.org/

Crockett, Z. (2016, June 15). *What happens after a mass shooting? Americans buy more guns.* Retrieved from

VOX: http://www.vox.com/2016/6/15/11936494/after-mass-shooting-americans-buy-more-guns

Detert, J. R., & Burris, E. R. (2016, January-February). Can Your Employees Really Speak Freely? *Harvard Business Review.*

Dollar, D., Fisman, R., & Gatti, R. (1999). *Are woman the "Fairer" Sex? Corruption and Women in Government.* The World Bank, Development Research Group. New York: The World Bank.

Duhigg, C. (2016, February 25). *What Google Learned From Its Quest to Build the Perfect Team.* Retrieved from www.nytimes.com: http://www.nytimes.com/2016/02/28/magazine/what-google-learned-from-its-quest-to-build-the-perfect-team.html

Edmondson, A. C. (2012). *Teaming.* San Francisco: Jossey-Bass.

Gallup. (2013). *State of the Global Workplace.* Washington: Gallup.

Gladwell, M. (2008). *Outliers.* New York: Little, Brown and Company.

Goffee, R., & Jones, G. (2007, March). Leading Clever People. *Harvard Business Review.*

Greer K. Gosnell, J. A. (2016). *A New Approach to an Age-Old Problem: Solving Externalities by Incentivising Workers Directly.* National Bureau of Economic Research. Cambridge: National Bureau of Economic Research.

Guinote, A., & Vescio, T. K. (2010). *The Social Psychology of Power.* New York: The Guilford Press.

Harter, J. K., Schmidt, F. L., Agrawal, S., Plowman, S. K., & Blue, A. (2016). *The Relationship Between Engagement at Work and Organizational Outcomes 2016 Q12® Meta-Analysis: Ninth Edition.* Washington: Gallup Inc.

HBR. (2012). *HBR Guide to Giving Effective Feedback.* Harvard Business Review.

Heen, S., & Stone, D. (2014, February). Find the Coaching in Criticism. *Harvard Business Review.*

Hofstede, G., Hofstede, G. J., & Minkov, M. (2010). *Culture and Organizations.* New York: McGraw Hill.

House, R. J., Hanges, P. J., Javidan, M., Dorfman, P. W., & Gupta, V. (2004). *Culture, Leadership and Organizations. The GLOBE Study of 62 Societies.* Thousand Oaks: Sage Publications Inc.

Keane, M. (1987). On retrieving analogues when solving problems. *Quarterly Journal of experimental Psychology*, pp. 29-41.

Kets de Vries, M. (2001). *The Leadership Mystique.* Harlow: FT Prentice Hall.

Kets de Vries, M. (2006). *The Leader on the Couch.* Chichester: John Wiley & Sons.

Kets de Vries, M. F. (2011). *Reflections on Groups and Organizations.* Chichester: John Wiley & Sons.

Kirk, A., & Dunford, D. (2016, June 29). *EU*

referendum: The claims that won it for Brexit, fact checked. Retrieved from The Telegraph: http://www.telegraph.co.uk/news/2016/06/22/eu-referendum-fact-checking-the-big-claims1/

Kotter, J. P. (2011). *Leading Change.* Boston, Massachusetts, USA: Harvard Business School Publishing Corporation.

Lawrence, P., & Nohria, N. (2002). *Driven. How human nature shape our choices.* San Francisco: Jossey-Bass.

Linderbaum, B. A., & Levy, P. E. (2010, November). The Development of Validation of the Feedback Orientation Scale (FOS). *Journal of Management, 36*(6), 1372-1405.

Little, B. L. (2014). *Me, Myself and Us.* Philadelphia: Public Affairs.

Marcus, L. P. (2011, December 19). *RBS's board lessons.* Retrieved from Reuters: http://blogs.reuters.com/lucy-marcus/2011/12/19/rbss-board-lessons/

Medina, J. (2008). *Brain Rules.* Seattle: Pear Press.

Meyer, E. (2014). *The Culture Map.* New York: Public Affairs.

Millon, T. (2004). *Personality Disorders in Modern Life.* Hoboken: John Wiley & Sons.

Mishra, P., McCulloch, A., Handa, A., Dale, T., Hirst, G., & Catchpole, K. (2009, April). The effects of aviation-style non-technical skills training on technical performance and outcome in the operating theatre. *Quality & Safety Health Care*, 109-115.

Peters, S. (2013). *The Chimp Paradox.* New York: Penguin Group.

Samuels, S. (2014, November 25). A culture ratio is more important than a capital ratio. *Financial Times.*

Shermer, M. (2011). *The Believing Brain.* New York: Times Books.

Smith, M. E. (2002, 8 FEB). Success Rates for Different Types of Organisational Change. *Performance Improvement, 41*(1), pp. 26-33.

Stain, S. J., & Book, H. (2011). *The EQ Edge.* Mississauga: John Wiley & Sons Canada.

Sully de Luque, M. F., & Sommert, S. M. (2000, October). The Impact of Culture on Feedback-seeking Behavior: and Integrated Model and Propositions. *Academy of Management Review, 25*(4), 829-849.

Sutton, Hornsey, & Douglas. (2012). *Feedback.* New York: Peter Lang Publishing.

Syed, M. (2015). *Black Box Thinking: The Surprising Truth About Success.* London: John Murray .

The Economist. (2016, July 30). *Corporate Governance.* Retrieved from The Economist: http://www.economist.com/news/business-and-finance/21702553-faced-mounting-criticism-big-business-bosses-offer-some-sensible-governance-reforms

Turner, C. (2015, November 20). *www.huffingtonpost.com.* Retrieved from Huffpost Business: http://www.huffingtonpost.com/caroline-turner/unconscious-gender-bias-i_b_8603794.html

Van der Fluit, E. (2016, January 16). *Het Financieel Dagblad.* Retrieved from Captains, hoed u voor het oerconflict: http://fd.nl/profiel/1135377/captains-hoed-u-voor-het-oerconflict

Wagner, R., & Harter, J. K. (2006). *12: The Elements of Great Managing.* New York: Gallup Press.

Walker, D. (2009). *A review of corporate governance in UK banks and other financial industry entities.* HM Treasury. London: HM Treasury.

Zenger, J., & Folkman, J. (2013, March 15). The Ideal Praise-to-Critisism Ratio. *Harvard Business Review.*

NOTES

1 (Van der Fluit, 2016)

2 (James K. Harter, 2016)

3 (Gallup, 2013)

4 (Adkins, Employee Engagement in U.S. Stagnant in 2015, 2016)

5 (Adkins, What Millennials Want From Work and Life, 2016)

6 (Sutton, Hornsey, & Douglas, 2012, p. 325)

7 (Geert Hofstede, 2010, pp. 5-7)

8 (Paul Lawrence, 2002, pp. 55-148)

9 (Samuel Bendahana, 2015)

10 (David Dollar, 1999)

11 (Samuels, 2014)

12 (Walker, 2009)

13 (The Economist, 2016)

14 (CorpGov-SVC, 2016)

15 (Sutton, Hornsey, & Douglas, 2012, p. 129)

16 (Ashley Kirk, 2016)

17 (Crockett, 2016)

18 (Peters, 2013)

19 (Millon, 2004, p. 67)

20 (Syed, 2015)

21 (Sutton, Hornsey, & Douglas, 2012, p. 130)

22 (Robert J. House, 2004)

23 (Robert J. House, 2004, p. 348)

24 (Eric M. Anicich, 2015)

25 (Little, 2014, p. 29)

26 (Robert J. House, 2004, pp. 348-349)

27 (Turner, 2015)

28 (Jack Zenger, 2013)

29 (Bushe, 2010, pp. 182-183)

30 (Rodd Wagner, 2006, p. 52)

31 (Greer K. Gosnell, 2016)

32 (Duhigg, 2016)

33 (James R. Detert, 2016)

34 (Sutton, Hornsey, & Douglas, 2012, p. 247)

INDEX

D

E

F

36455542R00123

Printed in Poland
by Amazon Fulfillment
Poland Sp. z o.o., Wrocław